D0549493

A Paradiso Year

A Paradiso Year

Spring & Summer Cooking

DENIS COTTER

PHOTOGRAPHY BY JÖRG KÖSTER

DESIGN AND ART DIRECTION BY JOHN FOLEY

ATRIUM

First published in 2005 by

Atrium

(an imprint of Cork University Press)

Youngline Industrial Estate

Pouladuff Road

Togher

Cork

Ireland

© Denis Cotter 2005

Photographs © Jörg Köster 2002–2003

Designed by John Foley at Bite, Cork
Set in Adobe Minion

Repro by The Scanning Shop, Dublin
Printed in Great Britain by Butler & Tanner.

British Library Cataloguing in Publication data
A CIP catalogue record for this book is available from the British Library.

Denis Cotter has asserted his moral right, under the Copyright and Related Rights Act 2000, in this work.

ISBN 0-9535353-6-3
A CIP record for this publication is available from the Library of Congress.

For all Atrium books visit www.corkuniversitypress.com

Visit Café Paradiso on the internet at www.cafeparadiso.ie

Introduction

Spring … here it comes again … that time when, it is said, a young man's fancy turns to love. Or to asparagus, if your mind is that way inclined. Time to cast off heavy winter coats and lift our heads from the months of biting cold. Time to pack away our indoor diversions, unbatten the metaphorical hatches. Dig out a favourite t-shirt and feel the first, faint warmth of the sun. Gardeners and growers, locked up for months with only indoor plotting and scheming for respite, take to the softening earth like pagans. Even the most sedate, urban, concrete-bound among us feels the lightening of a load, a creeping sense of optimism. Spring is, year after year, a time of renewal, a chance to start again.

Plants, too, take a gamble on feeling the ground soften a little, pushing up tender, hopeful shoots. For those, and I must admit to being one, who don't grow food but love to cook and eat, spring gives us foods bursting with new vitality and vivid energy. After months of heavy dishes made from roots and 'cupboard food', we have the first shoots of spring greens and sprouting broccoli, wild garlic, rocket; and later, asparagus, artichokes, broad beans: I have my obsessions – you may have your own list. The plants of spring change how we cook, lightening our dishes, giving them a high, delicate sweetness and vibrancy.

Where spring is full of promise and hope, summer is the big payoff of the growing season. When it happens – and in this climate, it doesn't always – summer is the easiest time to cook. The variety and quality of produce is such that it often needs little more than careful handling and pairing with the right ingredients. At the height of the season, we feast on so many varieties at one time – tomatoes, peppers, courgettes and their delicate flowers, chard and all of the beans and peas. But if there is a highlight to the bounty of summer, it is surely the delicate, fragrant fruits that feed our memories as much as our bellies. Cherries alone would make the season worthwhile, yet they are followed gluttonously by sun-ripened strawberries and raspberries, the almost sinful pleasures of peaches, and intensely fragrant melons. Shop, or pick carefully and you can make your own memories.

Therein lies the crux of the matter, and the essence of why we are returning to a greater emphasis on seasonal foods. Eating seasonally is not a diet, or a new food fad. It is ancient and simple. It is also an attempt to retake the pleasure of eating well, in the true sense. And the pleasure of eating foods at their best, in their best season, is only available to us if we leave them to their time. It is more than an accident that some of the most perfect combinations of foods are those of the same season, or those that pass each other on the rise and fall of each one's unique seasonal curves. Watercress and fresh spring sheep's cheese, peaches and lavender, tomatoes and basil, peas and mint, pumpkins and hazelnuts, peppers and summer chard. These foods almost take care of their own menus and recipes.

Given that foods cooked and eaten in season are likely to be grown (relatively) locally, be fresher, probably requiring less chemical interference, there is a good chance they will be cheaper and taste better. Taste is the main pleasure we get from food, but it is not the whole story. Fast food, junk food, factory pizza, cheap replica vegetables, all these can titillate your taste buds, but it is often a grim pleasure.

Cooking with an emphasis on seasonal produce, our pleasure in food is increased by the cycle of feasting, letting go and looking forward. This affects us greatly in Café Paradiso. I suppose I should say that we allow it to affect us. When the first

A PARADISO YEAR INTRODUCTION

asparagus – or broad beans or baby artichokes – shows up, we put on a starter that uses just a little of it. Then, as the season kicks in, we increase the amount used until it is all over the menus. I admit it can be frightening when the season wanes and we eventually, often reluctantly, let it go. Indeed, we sometimes scramble around shamelessly trying to squeeze one last week out of it, until we pull ourselves together, realising there is so much fabulous summer produce on the horizon. The first delivery of chard is so much better than the last ragged bunch of asparagus. Now, every time the asparagus season teases its way in, it is as exciting as the last time – but then so too is the arrival of the first autumn pumpkins or leeks.

Focusing attention on certain foods only when they are at their best, and in season, increases our awareness of them. And paying attention is the first step to enjoyment and pleasure. If we shop with awareness of the source and seasonality of foods, and bring home foods that excite our sense of expectation, we will eat well. When we carelessly consume poor, flavourless versions of extraordinary things like peaches or tomatoes, when supermarket shopping has made them into mere dull, weekly habits, they become debased in our minds, and we think nothing of them. There is no pleasure there.

Its not always easy to even grasp the notion of the seasonality of food, especially if you shop in supermarkets. It seems to be a great fear of these outlets that if they don't have a large quantity of every product on their shelves every day of the year, that you will go somewhere else to get it. The increasing truth is that you have become so bored with eating poor out-of-season, mass-produced, flown-across-the-hemispheres imitations of asparagus, peaches, melons and beans that you are already going elsewhere. You are looking to buy real food from the man who grew it, or the man whom you trust and who knows the man who grew it. There is a growing disillusionment with the cheap, plentiful but dull food that has been the result of the mass-production systems of the second half of the twentieth century. Well-intended as the drive for cheap food was, it tore apart our relationship with food and left us feeling alienated and unable to satisfy our complex appetites. It is telling that the renewed interest in buying from producers at markets is being driven by consumers need to make contact, as much as by producers need to find a market. The need to repair our relationship with food is also part of the motivation behind the Slow Food Movement. Yet, the Movement's guiding principle is to strive to restore the right to pleasure in food, realising that real pleasure cannot be had in a damaged relationship.

All of these shifts in the food culture are inter-locked and working in the same direction. We want to understand our food, and to know that it has a time and a place, perhaps even a face. In essence, we want to reclaim the rich and complex, but ultimately simple, pleasure of eating well.

I hope that the recipes in this book help you to cook well but, equally, I hope that they encourage you to shop well. Better still, grow your own!

About the recipes

This is not intended to be a comprehensive collection of recipes. I haven't gathered up all the recipes I could think of for every vegetable I could identify. There are many books, written by more knowledgeable people, that are far closer to being authoritative manuals of vegetable cooking, of which two of my favourites are Alice Waters' *Chez Panisse Vegetables* and Digby Law's *A Vegetable Cookbook*. Instead, I have tried to use a small number of recipes to give a sense of the variety of dishes and styles that each vegetable can be used in. The vegetables are most, but not all, of my favourites over the course of a year. There are one or two vegetables missing that I simply didn't use much of in that particular year. It happens. Some years, some vegetables just drift by outside my focus. And some years, crops of vegetables are bountiful and beautiful; next year, it's a washout.

The recipes of each primary vegetable are grouped together, and the vegetables are arranged in a seasonal order, flowing through the year. 'Order' may be the wrong word here. The book was written through one year of seasons, and the layout derives from the order in which the vegetables came to me. Some vegetables have very long seasons, others flit by like butterflies. In my interpretations of the seasons, I buy produce primarily from local growers, but supplement and stretch the seasons with produce from other parts of the country and Europe. Hence, broad beans appear in the book in spring, when I first get them from a French organic grower, even though in a bad year the pods won't show a bulge in Ireland until mid summer. Black kale finds itself slotted into early summer, although research suggests it is naturally a vegetable of early winter in north Italy. However, my first grateful sighting of it each year is much earlier, and it is far too beautiful to be turned away.

If we were to do the same book in another year, rest assured the vegetables would, by their own or their growers single-minded stubbornness, show up in a slightly different order. I like this. It is much more stimulating to be reacting to the availability of produce than to be writing menus first and phoning in orders to make them happen.

Besides, I wanted the flow of the book to reflect the reality of seasonal changes. I've never been comfortable with the neat compartmentalisation of the year into four even-sized seasons. I sometimes argue that there are probably seven, but when I tried to tie the recipes to these, they still didn't fit. It's not really possible, but often done, to put a menu together at the start of each of the four official seasons using ingredients that are all present at the start and end of the 'season'. In spring, you would have no asparagus at the start and no sprouting broccoli at the end; in summer there would be no peppers, peaches or beans until halfway through or later. The reality is that vegetables are unaware of our breakdown of the year and show up in their own good time and in a raggle-taggle order. In Café Paradiso, I like to think that there has only ever been one menu. Rather than throwing it out at the end of August, for example, to be replaced by the 'Autumn' menu, that one menu responds to the ebb and flow of the vegetables through the year. They come and go one or two at a time, and the menu follows suit, changing a little here and there every now and again.

While some of the recipes in this collection are frequent features of the Café Paradiso menu, and are complex and conscious of their appearance, as restaurant food must be, most were devised at home and are intended for regular home use.

Some are little more than simple ways to prepare vegetables, and these are obviously open to personal interpretation. They can be simple dinners, side dishes or the starting point for something more elaborate. The recipes are always about the primary vegetable, and if a recipe pairs a vegetable with a spice or a cheese, chances are those two will be good together in any context. Take what you want from the recipes. I hope they are useful as reference points as much as definite instructions.

Don't undermine your precious vegetables with poor support. You should be just as fussy about your oils, vinegars, cheeses, flours, grains and so on. Unless something else is specified in a recipe, 'olive oil' always means a good extra virgin one; 'balsamic vinegar' means a traditionally aged one from Modena, at least five years old; 'butter' means nothing less than real butter, and do try to use Irish butter – it has a richness of flavour I've never come across anywhere else.

Although this may seem a little uptight, many of the recipes give very specific instructions on chopping and slicing vegetables. This is not just for appearances; how the vegetable is cut affects how it cooks as well as the final texture and character of the dish. Two of the greatest sins in vegetable cooking are using random combinations of 'mixed veg' and careless cutting. Don't always cut a vegetable the same way: the thin diagonal slice of carrot used in a stirfry will obviously be hopeless for roasting. You don't always have to follow my cutting methods exactly; but when you approach a vegetable with a knife, stop for a second or two to think about the final dish. Try to get a clear sense of what you want to end up with, and then decide how to cut the vegetable to suit the dish.

Finally, all quantities in the recipes are net values; that is after all peeling and trimming – the amount, in other words, that you are putting in the pan.

Happy cooking.

Late Spring

rocket

asparagus

rhubarb

artichoke

broad beans

spinach

Rocket salad with avocado, spring onion, garlic croûtons and pecorino

A salad of rocket leaves is as frequent a part of feeding-time in our house as potatoes or bread. Most of the time it is simply a case of putting a bowl of leaves on the table close to a bottle of olive oil and a little bottle of balsamic vinegar with a clever home-made sprinkling mechanism. That way, the rocket is eaten before, during and after the meal, depending on your mood and the make-up of the main dish. Lightly dressed rocket is a great foil for rich food, adding that essential balance of freshness and pungency. Occasionally, we might dress the rocket up as a first course, and this version is only one of many possibilities. All the rocket needs is some olive oil, balsamic vinegar and one or two of a range of ingredients such as roasted baby beets, pinenuts, dried tomatoes, cherry tomatoes, broad beans, grilled asparagus, soft cheeses like fresh sheep's cheese or buffalo mozzarella, and so on.

A hard, salty cheese like pecorino is the perfect partner for rocket, but, if you can't get, or don't like, pecorino, use a cheese you do like.

FOR FOUR:

2 slices day-old bread
100mls olive oil
2 cloves garlic
3 spring onions
200–300g rocket
1 large avocado
2 tablespoons balsamic vinegar
salt and pepper, to taste
pecorino, or other hard cheese, for shaving

Brush the bread with a little of the olive oil, and then toast it lightly in a low oven (about 120°C/250°F). Rub the toast with the garlic before cutting it into small pieces.

Slice the spring onion very thinly on a long diagonal. Put the rocket in a bowl, add the spring onion and some of your croûtons.

Slice the avocado into long pieces and, if the flesh is firm enough, add it to the bowl. If the avocado seems too soft to survive being handled, leave it out of the mixed salad and simply tuck the slices into the individual plates of salad later. Sprinkle over the balsamic vinegar and the rest of the olive oil, add a little salt and pepper, and toss the salad gently a few times. Share out the salad and use a vegetable peeler to shave thin slivers of cheese over each serving.

Rigatoni with rocket, broad beans, cherry tomatoes, olives and fresh cheese

Rocket adds a little spicy kick and the tang of fresh greenery to a pasta dish, but only if you don't cook it too much. In fact, don't cook it at all, but stir it into the cooked pasta just before you serve. The first time I cooked rocket, in a potato cake with a clever hidden filling, I felt very pleased with myself in a modernist kind of way, pushing back the boundaries of cooking and all that jazz. That was fine until, one evening, a wise and kind experienced hand at the restaurant business in Cork ate it and said that the dish was nice but I could have saved myself some money by using grass or a few weeds for all the flavour or character of rocket that survived the cooking. Actually, he wasn't as cruel as that, but he was genuinely concerned at my waste of both money and fine produce. So, rocket is definitely one of those vegetables that gives a cook the challenge of conflicting interests: the contradiction between the cook's need to give the impression of doing something clever, and the knowledge that the vegetable is at its best with the minimum of interference – no more is required than a little teasing out of its best qualities and the careful selection of partner ingredients.

This pasta dish has the lightness, simplicity and bright pungency of spring, which is why I like to serve fresh cheese with it – made to be consumed young, fresh cheese also has those springtime characteristics of lightness and delicacy. I alternate between Knockalara sheep's cheese and Oisín goats' cheese crottins; you may have your own favourites, and ricotta, mascarpone or any mild soft cheese will be fine.

FOR FOUR:

450g rigatoni

4 spring onions

4 cloves garlic

100g cherry tomatoes

12 kalamata olives

120mls olive oil

4 tablespoons cooked broad beans

black pepper and salt, to season

100g rocket

100g fresh cheese, from goats', sheep's or cows' milk

Bring a large pot of water to a boil and cook the pasta until just tender. Drain it and return it to the pot. Meanwhile, chop the spring onions into long diagonal pieces. Slice the garlic. Halve the tomatoes; stone the olives and chop them lengthways into halves or quarters. Heat a generous amount of olive oil in a wide pan and cook the onion and garlic gently for a minute. Add the tomatoes, olives and broad beans and cook for one minute more until the tomatoes break down a little. Add just a splash of water to the pan to pick up all of the juices, then tip the contents into the pasta pot with another generous glug of olive oil, a generous seasoning of black pepper and a little salt. Heat the pasta through briefly, then stir in the rocket. Serve the pasta and crumble some cheese over each portion.

Avocado and rocket risotto with shavings of Oisín goats' cheese and a lemon chilli oil

Hard, mature goats' cheese is a rare enough thing, I suppose. It needs a careful hand, and a good goatkeeper, to make it as a civilised and sophisticated cheese rather than a pungent and smelly challenge to the palate. Rose and Rochus of Oisín Farm near the Cork/Limerick border, make a sublime gouda-style cheese that, in its youth, melts beautifully and has a mild taste with just a hint of goat. At eight or nine months, however, the cheese has hardened, even taking on some of the crystalline texture of mature Parmesan. All aspects of the flavour have deepened: the cheese has dried and become creamier, sweeter and richer on the tongue, yet the goaty element is still in balance. Shavings peeled from a freshly cut cheese add a perfect finishing touch to a risotto, pasta or a salad of strong character.

Rocket risotto is a fine combination, a little bit of peppery spirit in the king of comfort foods. But avocado? Some people look at me strangely the first time I suggest they put avocado in the risotto, and in fairness I wouldn't go chucking it into any old risotto. It is a particularly good companion to rocket, in salads as well as here. The avocado is added at the end so that it warms through but doesn't get heated to the point where it could become bitter. Take the trouble to source ripe but firm Haas avocados. They seem to ripen more evenly, and have a richer, full-fat texture. This is important when heating an avocado, as watery varieties become bitter at the mere sign of heat.

The lemon chilli oil used in this recipe, and the basic model chilli oil, is well worth having round the house, as a table condiment or to use in cooking. I don't like to encourage chilli addicts, or to enter macho chilli-eating contests, but sometimes you need to cook dishes for people with less kick than you would like and a little bowl of chilli oil on the table gives everyone great flexibility in the matter.

FOR FOUR:

FOR BASIC CHILLI OIL:
1 litre fruity olive oil
fresh or dried chillies (e.g. 20 bird's eye or 2 habaneros)

FOR THE LEMON CHILLI OIL:
200mls chilli oil (see above)
juice and rind of 1 lemon

To make a basic chilli oil, take a small amount, say 200mls, of fruity but not peppery olive oil. Chop or grind some fresh or dried chillies, maybe 20 bird's eye or two habaneros, and add these to the oil. Heat the oil gently for a couple of minutes, but don't quite boil it. Off the heat, add a litre of the same olive oil. Leave this to rest for a couple of hours – a day would be better – then test the oil. You may need to dilute it further, especially for table use, though a hot oil for cooking is fine, if your self-control is good. You can either sieve out the chillies, pour the oil off them into another container, or leave them to settle on the bottom – dried chillies will be fine left in, fresh ones may deteriorate.

Now, to make lemon chilli oil, take a small amount of the oil, say 200mls, as it is impossible to blend smaller amounts, add the lemon juice and rind, and use a hand blender to blend the two. The oil should thicken to a nice pouring consistency, though it might separate again later, in which case simply blend it again just before you use it.

FOR THE RISOTTO:

*1200mls vegetable stock
(see page 144)*

60g butter

60mls olive oil

*320g risotto rice, such as
arborio or carnaroli*

*1 bunch spring onions,
chopped*

4 cloves garlic, chopped

120mls dry white wine

60g Parmesan, grated

1 large avocado

100g rocket

salt and pepper, to season

*80g mature, hard goats'
cheese*

Bring the stock to the boil in a pot and keep it at a very low simmer. Meanwhile, melt one tablespoon of the butter with one spoon of the olive oil. Throw in the rice and stir it well to coat the grains with oil. Cook the rice gently for ten minutes, stirring often, then add the spring onion and garlic, and cook for one more minute. Pour in the wine, bring it to the boil quickly, then simmer until the wine is absorbed. Now add a ladle or cup of the stock, about 150mls, and continue to simmer, stirring often until it is all but absorbed. Add another cup of stock, and carry on absorbing, stirring and adding stock until the rice is almost cooked. Take care that the stock going into the rice pot is at a boil and, therefore, not interrupting the cooking of the rice. Test individual grains – the rice

should be cooked through but firm, while the stock has become a little creamy and is almost completely absorbed. When the risotto reaches this stage, take it off the heat and stir in the rest of the butter and olive oil and the Parmesan. Quickly chop the flesh of the avocado into large dice, coarsely chop or tear the rocket and add these to the risotto. Season well with salt and pepper.

Spoon the risotto on to plates, and use a vegetable peeler to shave slivers of the goats' cheese over it. Drizzle a little of the lemon-chilli oil around the fringes. Leave the oil and the lump of cheese on the table for those who like more kick than comfort in their dinner.

Grilled asparagus with salt flakes and rosemary aioli

Grilled asparagus is the simplest and, in my opinion, the nicest way to cook this finest of spring delicacies – the vegetable that epitomises the point of seasonal eating. You can get it out of season these days, but only from the other hemisphere, whichever one you don't live in, and doesn't it taste sad? The flavour of asparagus is so delicate, so elusive and yet so in-your-face when it's right. Asparagus is perfectly of its time, and that's why we feast on it for the short time it is with us.

For every time you dress asparagus up in fine recipes during the season, you should eat it this way at least twice, simply grilled, with or without the aioli. Don't just go grilling the first bunch you find this year, though. To serve thin asparagus with aioli, it would be better to lightly steam or boil it for no more than one minute, just enough to change it from raw to cooked. Grilling works best for fine big, fat spears. The outside skin browns, crisps and caramelises a little while the inner flesh barely cooks, retaining its inherent moist sweetness. I think maybe cookbooks sometimes over-encourage people to search out thin, elegant asparagus (come to think of it, asparagus isn't the only vegetable to suffer that fate) and I think there may be a little snobbish disdain for the bigger spears. I don't see it like that at all. The smaller, thinner spears are wonderful in salads and as crudités; and in risotto and pasta, hardly cooked at all but thrown in at the end for the last seconds of cooking. But to take on grilling or roasting, or in dishes with the flavours of strong cheese, you need a bigger asparagus, where there is enough body to give a contrast between the delicate, sweet flesh and the cooked green skin. The most important thing when buying asparagus is to check its condition and freshness. It is best if the heads are firm and fairly closed, but the other end is a better barometer. Those plastic or paper sheets around the shins of the asparagus, and the often-too-tight elastic bands, can hide old age and bad condition. Take a look below the knee-line and at the base of the stalks – they should be fresh and crisp, not dried up or beginning to show mould, even if the tops look fine.

FOR FOUR:

2 sprigs rosemary
300mls oil
5 cloves garlic
2 tablespoons olive oil
2 egg yolks
half teaspoon hot mustard
salt and pepper, to season
juice of half lemon

2 bunches asparagus
salt flakes

First make the rosemary oil. Pull the leaves of rosemary from their stems and put them in a small pan with 100mls of olive oil. Bring this slowly to a boil, remove the pan from the heat and leave to infuse for at least 30 minutes, much longer if possible. Strain the infused oil into the remaining 200mls of olive oil. Rosemary oil keeps very well and is very useful, so it is a good idea to make much larger quantities than this.

Snip the ends off the garlic cloves and put them on a small oven tray, drizzled with a little olive oil. Roast them in a low to medium oven for about 15 minutes until the garlic is soft. Squeeze the garlic from its skin into a food processor with the egg yolks and mustard. Blend these for a full minute before beginning to drizzle in the rosemary oil, then continue to add the oil slowly until the aioli

has taken on a thickish dip-like consistency. Check the flavour of the aioli, add salt and pepper, taste it again and add some or all of the lemon juice, to your liking.

Heat a grill to a high temperature. Snap the ends off the asparagus spears, and lay them close together on a tray. Drizzle some olive oil over the asparagus and put the tray under the grill. Cook the asparagus until it begins to colour a little in places, but remains firm – this should take only three or four minutes. Pile the grilled asparagus on to a serving dish and scatter over some flaked salt.

Serve with a generous bowl of the aioli to dunk the spears in.

Asparagus, caramelised onion and Knockalara sheep's cheese tart

Cooking with Knockalara sheep's cheese can sometimes make me nervous and unsure. Oh, it's a dream to use in salads, breaking off angular lumps from the wheel and tucking them into bitter salad leaves or wilted greens. It's a subtle, fresh cheese with a clean, slightly lemony zing that I fear will get lost in my big-flavoured cooking. Yet it often surprises me how that subtlety adds a touch of class to a dish I might have expected it to get lost in. And sometimes I pay attention to the subtlety of the cheese and keep my excesses in check. This tart is a simple affair, with little chance of the cheese getting lost. It is a natural-born partner to asparagus, in the way that foods of a season just seem so right for each other. That compatibility is at the heart of what I love about cooking seasonally. The foods of any one time of the year seem designed by nature to get along perfectly on the plate and in the pot. For example, if you do this tart with chopped watercress instead of asparagus, you will get the same fresh spikiness of spring. Do it with the strong, cabbage greens of a few weeks earlier in late winter/early spring and you might as well have used sour milk.

The tart doesn't really need embellishment, but I would often serve it with a sweetish sauce such as tomato pesto or a cherry tomato salsa, some new potatoes and a salad, perhaps even the watercress one on page 171.

The red onions will take about an hour to cook but they keep for a week or more and are very useful, so I would suggest you make a large batch the day before you make the tart.

You will need a pastry case 26cm in diameter.

FOR FOUR:

160g plain flour
large pinch salt
80g cold butter
40mls cold water

250g red onions
tablespoon olive oil
2 tablespoons brown sugar
2 tablespoons balsamic vinegar

1 bunch asparagus
150g Knockalara sheep's cheese
3 eggs
150mls cream
salt and pepper, to season

Sift the flour and salt, then cut in the butter. A food processor does this very efficiently, but remove the pastry to a bowl before stirring in the water with a few quick strokes. Shape the dough into a ball with your hands, flatten it gently and chill it for at least half an hour. Then roll the pastry to fit a 26cm pastry case and chill for a further half hour. Blind-bake the pastry case for about ten minutes at about 180°C/350°F.

Slice the red onions in half, then into thin slices. Cook them in a little olive oil, stirring often, until the onions are fully cooked and beginning to caramelise. Add the sugar and balsamic vinegar, and continue to cook until the onions are breaking down and the liquid is syrupy. Leave to cool.

Snap the ends off the asparagus and cook the spears in boiling water for two minutes. Break the cheese into small pieces. Beat the eggs and cream together and season with salt and pepper. Chop the asparagus spears into pieces about 1cm long and, setting aside the heads, mix them with the sheep's cheese. Spread a layer of caramelised onions in the pastry case and cover with the asparagus and sheep's cheese. Arrange the asparagus heads on top and pour over the custard. Bake in an oven at 180°C/350°F until the tart is just set, about 30 to 40 minutes. If you are using a fan oven, turn the fan off after the first ten minutes to allow the tart to cook without burning the top.

Fresh herb and feta omelette with warm asparagus, avocado and cherry tomato salsa

I've long had a secret desire to put omelettes on the restaurant menu, ever since I ate a perfect one in a café open to the street in Auckland one summer morning a year or ten ago. It was a concoction, filled with fashionable leaves and garnished with a salsa that included olive oil and a nice kick of chilli, and served almost lost at the bottom of a gigantic, wide and shallow dish. For all its flashy elements, it was also a perfectly executed omelette, soft and luscious. I remember it almost every time I beat a few eggs together for dinner. But that was a casual brunch menu – at Paradiso we don't do brunch, and somehow the omelette has lost its place on restaurant menus – mostly due to abuse, the usual tyrant, and long years of rubbery, watery frisbees made from factory eggs and plastic ham. One of these days… but probably not.

I don't claim to understand the scientific theory on the compatibility of asparagus and eggs, but it is one that works in many different ways – asparagus with scrambled eggs, soft-boiled eggs, hollandaise or aioli, and, of course, the omelette. Asked what I cook at home I sometimes fantasise about picking vegetables from my pristine plot, creating exquisite and intricate delicacies that are too difficult and spontaneous to reproduce in the restaurant. Often, I will go so far as to pass off these fantasies as truths, and later feel a mixture of guilt and mischievous glee. Sometimes, though, I will admit that dinner is most often pasta or eggs – simple, soul-reviving, Sunday-evening food. And in that territory, the omelette is king. A well-made omelette is a culinary double act. On the one hand, the most luxurious and decadent thing – your whole week's allowance of egg cholesterol with some butter or olive oil for good measure, maybe some cheese and a dollop of mashed or roast potatoes – yet, at the same time, the simplest, fastest, most fundamentally peasant kitchen-garden supper. Grab whatever number of eggs you can find, crack them into a pan, stir a bit and flip the thing on to a plate. Food.

The climactic scene in the movie *Big Night* is an omelette scene, and the first calm scene for some time. The two brothers, Primo and Segundo, cook and waiter, worn out from the extraordinary stresses of the day, meet in the kitchen and share some eggs. They call it an omelette, though in the Italian style it is just some beaten eggs fried in a pan – no lifting, flipping or filling. I think I had hoped to see a pristine demonstration of the art of the omelette, and was a little disappointed the first time I saw the film. But it's not about technique. As the simple, slow and careful movements are carried out to prepare and cook the eggs, the brothers, who had in the preceding madness fallen out, come back to each other, a sense of sanity and peace returns, and you realise that this is the true power of food: to bring people together. Earlier in the evening, the brothers had given intense pleasure to a wide range of characters, bringing the two together if only for one evening, with their flamboyant, labour-intensive and divinely flavoured restaurant food. But for their own coming together, that food would not have been enough. Sitting down to eight courses of rich food would have sparked more debate than reconciliation. No, for the brothers it had to be eggs, cooked in the family style, no questions asked. It is hard to imagine what other dish could have been used to facilitate the scene.

Speaking of technique, I re-read Elizabeth David on the matter of eggs recently, expecting to have confirmed what I thought I had learned from her. Instead, it turns out that I don't cook omelettes à la Ms David at all, and that she doesn't believe there is a proper way. She does, instead, allow for all manner of personal variations and encourages the ritualistic element of cooking, exactly the element that made the preparation of an omelette in *Big Night* such a redemptive experience. In essence, learn a comfortable way to do it, and do it often, so that it becomes a routine that brings you peace and pleasure.

   This recipe is for two. If you have more to feed, share it or cook a second omelette – it will only take two minutes if everything is ready.

FOR TWO:

6 spears asparagus
8 cherry tomatoes, halved
1 clove garlic, chopped
half a fresh chilli, deseeded and diced
2 tablespoons olive oil

4–5 eggs
2 tablespoons water
salt and pepper, to season
handful of fresh herbs (of two or three types, such as chives, parsley, thyme, tarragon, marjoram)
50g feta
butter or olive oil to coat pan

half an avocado

Snap the ends off the asparagus, chop the spears into pieces about 3cm long, and grill or steam these for a minute or two until just tender. Put the cherry tomatoes in a small pan over a low heat with the garlic, chilli and olive oil. Cook gently for two minutes until the tomatoes just begin to collapse, then remove from the heat and add in the asparagus. Do all of this just before cooking the omelette, then, when the omelette is cooked, a mere two minutes later, dice the avocado flesh and stir it gently into the warm salsa.

Crack the eggs into a bowl and beat them briefly just to break them up, then add two tablespoons of water, some salt and pepper. Chop the herbs, crumble the feta and set them at the ready. Heat a heavy flat pan to a high temperature (your omelette pan – the one you never use for anything else and always wipe out immediately with never a scour, scrape nor detergent near it). Brush the pan with a coating of butter or olive oil, pour in the beaten egg, give them a quick stir, tilt the pan towards you, then away, each time lifting the edge of the omelette to let the raw egg run under the cooked. Do this once or twice more, then scatter the ready-prepared herbs and feta over the centre of the omelette. Flip one-third of the omelette over the middle, then the other. Remove the pan from the heat and divide the omelette on to two plates. Spoon some of the salsa over each.

Rhubarb and glazed pecan crumble with a gingered rhubarb syrup

Rhubarb is the first fruit of the year – the only one to appear in spring – and it is greatly appreciated for its early showing. That said, it is not really a fruit at all, but the stalk of a leaf plant – a vegetable in fact. And it's certainly not sweet, but quite sour. Yet it is almost always cooked with sugar to make sweet dishes, which makes it an honorary fruit.

Rhubarb is a peculiarly old-fashioned food, which, I think, is best if treated in a fairly old-fashioned way. This recipe, a crumble, is a variation on a standard from another era, and the next most likely dishes to be made with rhubarb are equally simple and old-fashioned: stewed with custard, tarts and pies, fools and jams; the rhubarb and shortbread dish in *The Café Paradiso Cookbook* is simply a rejigged version of stewed rhubarb, biscuits and cream. I like to serve the gratins in individual portions by cooking them in steel rings. This is mainly for aesthetic reasons, but the rings also help to maintain the proportions between rhubarb and crumble, and I like to be able to serve a little extra syrup on the side. If you don't have rings or find all that too fussy, just layer the rhubarb and crumble into an oven dish and bake for longer.

Most rhubarb recipes begin by tossing chopped rhubarb with lots of sugar and cooking it gently. 'Gently' is important – rhubarb passes through the stage of being perfectly cooked and on to mushy in a timescale not much beyond the blink of an eye.

Of course, for every rhubarb lover there is another who can't stand the stuff, though I suspect that these unfortunate people may be carrying traumatic memories from childhood. In any case, it is on this love/hate aspect of rhubarb that I have based my philosophy on its place in restaurant menus. Simply, I believe that if you put a rhubarb dish on a menu (and you always should in spring) then it should have lots of rhubarb in it and should taste predominantly of rhubarb. The rhubarb haters won't go near any dish featuring the 'r' word on the menu, while rhubarb lovers will be inconsolably disappointed if they find that you led them on only to present them with a concoction with the merest scraping of rhubarb buried in the mix. No, they want rhubarb, you promised rhubarb, so it is best to satisfy their craving. And the truth of it is that, no matter what you do to trick out a rhubarb dish, nothing will please the true fan as much as a huge bowl of warm rhubarb and some homemade custard. Give in.

FOR THE SYRUP:

1 bunch rhubarb, 600g net weight

400g caster sugar

FOR THE CRUMBLE:

100g flour

30g light muscovado sugar

60g butter

half teaspoon ground ginger

30g caster sugar

1 teaspoon maple syrup

50g pecans

2 preserved ginger nuts

Chop the rhubarb into pieces 2cm or 3cm long, and put them in a large pot with the caster sugar. Bring this to a boil and simmer, covered, over very low heat for five minutes until barely tender. Carefully lift the rhubarb out with a slotted spoon, then strain the liquid through a fine sieve to get a clear juice.

Put the flour, muscovado sugar, butter and ground ginger into a food processor and blend in brief spurts to get a fine crumb-like texture. Spread the crumble on a baking tray and bake it at 180°C/350°F for five or six minutes until lightly toasted.

Put the caster sugar and maple syrup in a small pan over very low heat until the sugar is melted. Stir in the pecans and immediately spread them on an oven tray lined with parchment. Put the tray in a low oven, 120°C/250°F for 20 minutes. Leave the pecans to become dry and crisp. Stir them into the crumble.

Pile the rhubarb into an oven dish, or into individual steel rings, and scatter a layer of the crumble over the top, pressing it on gently. Bake at 180°C/350°F until the rhubarb is hot; about ten minutes for individual crumbles, longer for one large one.
While the crumble is cooking, put the rhubarb juice in a pan. Slice the ginger nuts thinly and add them to the juice, then simmer for five minutes until the juice has the consistency of a thin pouring syrup. If it becomes too thick, simply stir in a little water and simmer again. Allow the syrup to cool to room temperature again before serving it. Serve the crumble with a stream of the syrup poured around it, and some citrus ice cream, or just a dollop of fresh cream or mascarpone.

Grilled artichoke with roasted pepper and basil aioli

I first ate artichokes this way in a sleepy small town north of San Francisco. We were lunching in a courtyard restaurant on the corner of the square, and I ordered grilled artichoke just to see how you did it. It was so blindingly obvious when the dish arrived, dressed with a tomato salsa kind of thing, and it was a very pleasant way to spend half an hour. Between the artichoke, the sauvignon blanc and the general cowpoke ambience, we so fell under the spell of the town that we booked into the old colonial hotel on the opposite corner of the square – you know, lots of ancient dark wood, fine white linen, bourbon, moose heads and rifles on the stair landings – and were kept awake all night, first by 'hoons' cruising the streets, and then the refuse truck, which started work at an ungodly hour, reversing around tricky corners, only shortly after the lads had revved off home to bed. In the morning the town looked less romantic through bleary sleepless eyes, and we moved on.

You could say that this is a sort of inside-out version of the classic method of eating an artichoke by picking the leaves from the outside in and scraping off the edible flesh from the base of each leaf with the front teeth, until the prized heart is reached. In keeping with the impatience of modern living, this reversed recipe allows you to get at the prize first and go on picking at the outer leaves only as long as you can be bothered. Oh my god, I'm going off this dish even as I type it! For those of you who don't like to dive straight in but want to play mind games with your food, and I'm completely with you on this, pick and nibble the leaves from the inside out but leave the heart until last when it is fully exposed and uncluttered.

FOR FOUR TO FIVE:

2 red peppers
4 cloves garlic
2 egg yolks
1 small bunch basil
300mls olive oil
4 large artichokes
juice of half lemon
salt and pepper, to season

Put the peppers on a tray under a hot grill, turning them as necessary until their skins are blackened all over. Pop them into a paper bag until they are cool enough to handle. Nick the ends off the garlic cloves and put them in a low to medium oven until they become soft.

Peel the peppers, discard the seeds and put the flesh into a food processor. Squeeze the garlic from their skins into the processor too. Add the egg yolks, tear the basil and toss it in. Blend everything for two minutes, then pour in the olive oil in a thin, slow stream, until the aioli has the consistency of a mayonnaise or dip.

Cut the artichokes into halves, then into quarters. Use a small knife or a spoon to remove all of the hairy choke, and drop the pieces into a bowl of water to which you have added the juice of a lemon. Bring a pot of water to a boil and cook the artichoke pieces in it until just tender. Check their consistency by sticking a sharp knife into the thickest part of the base.

Just before serving, heat the grill, brush the artichokes with olive oil, season with salt and pepper, and cook the artichokes until lightly browned.

Serve three or four quarters each with a little bowl of aioli to dunk in.

Roasted globe artichoke with sheep's cheese and pinenuts, wilted greens and tomato pesto

For this, you will need large, wide, pale-green artichokes. You should be able to get artichoke bottoms with diameters of 6cm to 8cm, but in your search for large artichokes don't forget that the leaves should still be tightly closed – you want large ones, not old and overgrown. It is a lot of work preparing the artichokes, though you can get up quite a speed a few weeks into the season at a rate of 20 a day! Mind you, when a supplier came up with a late crop last autumn, I had to turn it down, fearing mutiny from my hard-working but fragile-spirited crew, who were certain they'd seen the last of these monsters for a few months. The real beauty of this dish is that the eaters of the artichokes will be overwhelmed with admiration for the person who has presented them with a ready-to-eat version of a vegetable they are usually obliged to work on at the table, picking one leaf out after another.

The filling is a variation on a combination I use in many dishes: sheep's cheese and pinenuts. They just seem so made for each other. I have used other fillings successfully but, as in all artichoke dishes, the important thing is to keep the additional flavours low-key, light and fresh, to allow the artichoke's strong but subtle character to shine through.

FOR FOUR:

FOR THE TOMATO PESTO:
100g sundried tomatoes
2 cloves garlic
300mls olive oil
salt and pepper, to season

Soak the sundried tomatoes for 20 minutes in enough warm water to cover them. Purée them in a food processor with the garlic, then pour in the olive oil, with the motor running, until you get a thick but pourable consistency. Season with salt and pepper.

4 large globe artichokes
juice of 2 lemons
25g pinenuts
200g sheep's cheese
a few leaves fresh basil
olive oil, as required
4 handfuls black kale, chard or spinach

Working with one artichoke, cut the artichoke stem about a centimetre from the base. Snap off the outer green leaves as close to the base as possible until the leaves revealed are a pale yellow-green shade right up to the widest part of the artichoke. Now cut the top from the artichoke at this widest part, and peel the tough outer green skin from the base. Finally, use a spoon to scoop out the hairy choke from the centre. This leaves you with a completely edible artichoke bottom. Drop each finished artichoke into cold water to which you have added the juice of one lemon – this will help to prevent discolouring. Bring a pot of water to the boil, add the juice of the other lemon and drop in the artichokes. Boil them until just tender; about ten minutes should do it but check by piercing one with a sharp knife – it should be firm but easily cut. Plunge the artichokes into cold water again to cool them and stop the cooking.

While the artichokes are cooking, lightly toast the pinenuts, crumble the cheese and mix it with the pinenuts, some chopped basil and a little salt and pepper.

Brush the artichokes with olive oil, season them, and roast them in a hot oven for about ten minutes, until they start to brown a little at the edges. Now, pile some of the cheese filling into each artichoke, leaving the filling loosely packed. Drizzle a little oil over the top and put them back in the oven for a few minutes to heat through. Just before you take the artichokes out of the oven, heat some more olive oil in a wide saucepan. Tear the greens into pieces, drop them in and stir over a high heat until they wilt and soften – an occasional splash of water will help. Season with salt and pepper, then place a small pile of greens on each of four plates. Put one artichoke on each pile and run a stream of pesto around the edge.

Broad bean salad with grilled haloumi, wild garlic, lemon-thyme oil and crispbreads

Broad beans crop up here because this is the time I associate them with, the time I first buy fresh organic broad beans. They come from Italy or the south of France, and I admit I take them as soon as I can get them, and even at that I've been hanging out for them for a few weeks. Local Irish organic broad beans don't kick in until mid-June, or mid-July in a bad year. This approach allows me to get a very long season with new young crops arriving every couple of weeks as the season moves up through Europe. We're all good Europeans now, and I've decided to apply that concept to seasonal food. The first broad beans are tiny and edible raw: through the season the beans grow larger and thicker-skinned, and they need longer cooking and sometimes peeling too. It's worth mentioning that frozen broad beans are generally very good quality, though I do believe you will appreciate the vegetable more if you prepare it from its pod rather than simply slitting a plastic bag.

Broad beans, or fava beans as they are known in other parts of the world, seem to divide that part of the population that pays them any attention: you either love and crave them or you hate them. Now, I am a fully paid-up member of the broad bean fan club and self-elected chairperson of the committee to encourage more broad bean eating, but I'm fascinated as much by the foods people hate as those that are loved. And while I can certainly understand people gagging at the thought of seaweeds, stinking mushrooms from dank forests, pickles… I can even understand phobias from childhood experiences – boarding-school parsnips or the texture of over-ripe bananas – but broad beans? Maybe it's just exaggeration and what people mean when they say those horrible things is merely that they don't really care too much for broad beans. I love everything about them, starting with the almost ludicrously luxurious soft white fur lining the inside of the pod, which makes shelling broad beans a more amusing job than you might expect.

This salad recipe is currently my favourite way to eat broad beans, but they are such a useful vegetable to have around; we put them in risotto and pasta, in stews, soups and ravioli; mash and salsas; and anything else we're cooking while broad beans are in the house.

This is a vibrant salad, full of the fresh sparkle and zing of lemon, lemon thyme and wild garlic. During spring, I use a lot of wild garlic – the variety with a grass-like leaf and a pretty white flower, like a white bluebell. If I forget to pick it at home, there is an emergency crop on the walk to work, growing on a grassy bank and even out of the supporting wall.

Haloumi is a fantastic food to work with – a cheese that can be fried without melting. The many brands available vary a little in quality (and in the rennet used) but most seem to be made with a combination of cows', goats' and sheep's milk, which is a few steps away from its origins in Cyprus as a sheep's milk cheese.

For years, I resisted the temptation to buy a lined griddle pan, having seen too many cookbooks full of pictures of fashionably striped food, and having eaten far too much restaurant food that cared more about its stripes than its taste. However, it became obvious that Johan, in Paradiso, would apply himself so much more enthusiastically to preparing this salad if I would fork out the measly €20 for a griddle pan to cook the haloumi on. I was right – he turned out perfect salads for the season; and, as always, he was right too – doesn't the haloumi look divine with its go-faster stripes, elevating peasant food to the heights of culinary fashion? Even the broad beans seem quite chuffed to be in such dandy company.

The flexible weight of broad beans in the recipe is dependent on the yield you get from the whole pods, and how much podding you are willing to do. I think shelling broad beans, and peas too, especially if done outdoors on a stoop in the sunshine, is guaranteed to make you feel in touch with nature in the way that sharpening a pencil with a knife makes grown men feel, well, manly. I don't enjoy peeling the beans though, and never would when they are young and small; nor do I like to tell other people to do it, as it can make the vegetable seem a chore too far, and I love broad beans too much to be putting people off them. However, the late-season monsters can be a bit thick-skinned, so do peel them if that offends you. However, I would always encourage you to eat the skin rather than give up broad beans.

FOR FOUR:

4 slices day-old bread
200mls olive oil
salt and pepper, to season
juice and rind of 1 lemon
2 sprigs fresh lemon thyme
300g broad beans, net weight
small bunch wild garlic
240g haloumi
some salad leaves

First make the crispbreads. Cut any crust off the bread, brush it all over with a little of the olive oil and season with salt and pepper. Bake the bread in a moderate oven, 180°C/350°F, until nicely browned and crisp all the way through. Break the slices into rough pieces about half the size of the haloumi slices.

Put the rest of the olive oil, lemon and thyme in a jug and use a hand blender to blend them to a slightly thick emulsion. If it separates after a while, blend it again just before you use it, and speak firmly but kindly to it.

Cook the shelled broad beans in boiling water until just tender. Drain them and cool them to warm, not cold, in cold water, then put them into a bowl. Chop the wild garlic and add it to the beans.

At the same time heat a griddle pan or a heavy frying pan to quite hot. Slice the haloumi block into six pieces and cut each of these in half diagonally. Brush the slices lightly with olive oil and place them on the hot pan. Cook over a high heat until lightly browned, then turn the slices to cook the other sides. Drop the haloumi into the bowl, put in an equal quantity of crispbread pieces and pour in enough of the oil to coat everything.

Serve the salad as it is, in the bowl, as part of a meal. To serve it as a starter, first put a little pile of salad leaves, such as rocket or mizuna, in the centre of each plate and spoon the salad over and around the leaves, taking care that everyone gets their fair share of haloumi.

Broad bean, feta and basil mash

I made this after a trek to London, the highlight of which was a broad bean mash I had in the River Café in London. I think theirs was made with a hard Italian cheese, pecorino maybe, and the basil was a later addition. I put the basil in to try to maintain a green colour without peeling the broad beans. It didn't really work, but when I relented on the peeling, I left the basil in because I'd come to love the taste of sunshine it brought to the mash. So, unfortunately, this is one broad bean dish where I would have to say that peeling is almost essential. There: I back-pedalled, I said 'almost'.

The mash is very useful as a rich accompaniment to many dishes, though you should think of it as a relish more than a vegetable dish. I love a dollop of it on a simple omelette or pancake; it's great on toast or bruschetta or with grilled polenta and salad. It doesn't keep well, but it rarely gets the chance anyway.

You will need about a kilo of broad bean pods to get 400g of beans.

FOR FOUR:

400g shelled broad beans
150g feta cheese
50g basil leaves
50mls olive oil

Pop the broad beans from their pods and cook them in boiling water until just tender. Cool the beans in cold water, then peel them by squeezing them individually between your fingers. Place the beans in a food processor with the feta, a generous handful of basil and a generous splash of olive oil. Blend the mixture in short bursts to get a rough mash. Season with salt and black pepper, though salt may be unnecessary with the feta. Use the mash at room temperature.

Broad beans with olive oil, marjoram and garlic

A simple way to serve broad beans as a side dish, combining them with flavours they love. It can be served hot or at room temperature. Marjoram doesn't get a lot of exposure these days, being overshadowed by its better-known but very similar cousin, oregano. The simple combination can also be used as the base for a more elaborate dish – with the addition of other vegetables after the cooking, such as tomatoes and asparagus or artichokes – or a warm salad, by scattering the beans over some salad leaves.

FOR FOUR:

300g broad beans
2 spring onions
6 cloves garlic
2 tablespoons olive oil
a few sprigs marjoram
salt and pepper, to season

Pop the broad beans from their pods and place them in a pan with just enough water to almost cover them. Slice the spring onions, chop the garlic roughly and add both to the pan with the olive oil. Bring this to a boil and simmer, covered, until the beans are tender, which should take about five to ten minutes, depending on their age and size. The water should evaporate; if it doesn't, simply turn up the heat and boil it off quickly. Add in the marjoram and seasoning and serve.

Ravioli of pinenuts, currants and Knockalara sheep's cheese in a lemon-thyme cream, with spinach and sundried tomato

I've just realised how much I use these flavours together. Knockalara sheep's cheese… pinenuts… lemon… thyme… spinach… tomato. Not always all at the same time, though, as they appear here. Well, I've given a few moments' thought to fiddling about with the recipe to disguise my predictable nature, to give off more of an air of maverick spontaneity and a diverse range of ideas. But then some other recipe would be swanning around your kitchen while my favourite version would be sulking at home in Paradiso, a reject, almost-wanted. So, then, here is another in an ongoing series of recipes featuring sheep's cheese, pinenuts, spinach, lemon, thyme and tomato. Oh, and currants. I love currants, the runts of the dried-fruit world. I'll admit there's an awful lot of gnarled tasteless droppings sold as currants, but get a supply of the best organic currants you can find and you have little pinpricks of concentrated sweet fruit. They add a lovely edge to these ravioli where their bigger cousins would be flabby intruders. I don't soak the currants for this recipe, but I do sometimes soak them to add to salads, and it always bewilders me when a diner asks for the salad without the currants – I mean, how offensive or scary can a currant be? Do give them a chance.

FOR FOUR:

4 halves sundried tomatoes

2 tablespoons pinenuts

200g sheep's cheese

1 tablespoon finest organic currants

2 sheets fresh pasta, approx 16cm x 60cm

150mls light stock (see page 144)

150mls white wine

rind and juice of 1 lemon

400mls cream

1 sprig lemon thyme

salt and pepper, to season

100g fresh spinach

Put the sundried tomatoes in a bowl for 20 minutes with just enough warm water to cover them, then drain and slice them into long thin strips.

Lightly toast the pinenuts, then chop them coarsely. Don't grind them, you don't want powder here, you want pieces of pinenut, half-nuts and suchlike. Crumble the cheese and gently mix in the pinenuts and currants.

Lay the pasta on a work surface and cut out two sets of circles, one slightly larger than the other, 12 of each size. From the size of pasta sheet specified, one circle of 8cm and one of 7cm would be perfect, but do whatever best suits the pasta size and your cutting equipment. One of those sets of pastry cutters with Russian doll-like ever-decreasing metal rings inside each other is ideal. Take a small-ish amount of the filling, small but as much as you think the parcel will hold… perhaps a rounded teaspoonful… roll it into a ball and place it in the centre of one of the smaller circles of pasta. Brush the visible part of the pasta circle with water and place one of the larger pieces on top. Now press the edges together firmly while, at the same time, taking care not to leave any air pockets inside the parcel. Repeat this with the rest of the parcels – you need three each for a starter, more for a main course.

Bring the stock, wine and lemon to a boil in a pan, and simmer until the volume is reduced by half. Add the cream and thyme, and simmer for a few minutes until the sauce thickens to a nice pasta-coating consistency – try some on the back of a wooden spoon to get an idea. Season carefully with salt and pepper. Keep the sauce warm, or make it before you start to cook the ravioli and reheat it gently.

Bring a large pot of water to a boil and drop in the ravioli. If you think the parcels might be overcrowded, do two batches. As with all pasta, the only way to decide that it's cooked is to test it. Nick a tiny bit off one of the ravioli and taste it. Remove the ravioli with a slotted spoon and put them in a bowl with a little olive oil to prevent them sticking to each other. If you do two batches, tip the first one back into the pot just as the second batch is cooked and remove the lot in half a minute.

Cook the spinach in the same water while you transfer the ravioli to warm plates. Drain the spinach and chop it into slices similar to the tomatoes. Strew a few of these and a few of the tomato slices over the ravioli, then pour a generous amount of the lemon-thyme sauce over each portion.

Almond pastry galette of wilted spinach, Knockalara sheep's cheese and crushed potato with tomato-cardamom relish

The foundation, in every sense, of this elegant dish is the way the layers of pastry and ground almonds are put together to give a very crisp, puffed-up finish. There are three pastries, each of three layers, so the final effect is of lightness and a crisp, airy texture. The layers are cooked separately and assembled on the plate, which helps to keep this crisp texture all the way to the table. The filling is a very simple and very traditional mixture of spinach and sheep's cheese. This approach came about after a long abstinence from filo pastry. I had become uncomfortable with it, having read a piece by a Turkish cook, I think, in which he insisted that filo pastry's natural affinity was with honey and nuts, and that the characteristic multiple layering would only work when there were very few, and very dry, ingredients between the layers, i.e. honey and nuts. He finished by invoking the gods, some gods or other, to keep filo pastry away from 'creative' chefs, and he didn't use those words in a complimentary way. It made me look at what I was doing with the pastry, and where I had learned to use it. On the positive side, we came up with a very good baklava recipe of about ten layers of honey, nuts and rosewater, which has been on the menu ever since.

There is one more layer underneath the pastry, which is not strictly necessary – one of crushed potato flavoured with coriander seeds. This is loosely based on my father's speciality, his one signature dish, known simply as 'Dad's fried potatoes' to distinguish them from my mother's more polite and more correct version of potato slices carefully fried to crisp on both sides. His would only be served after a long Sunday afternoon's rambling and strenuous cowboy and Indian carry-on. Where my recipe uses halfway floury rooster potatoes, he used the leftover ultra-floury ones from Sunday lunch; where I use olive oil, he used the white lard scooped off the top of a bowl in the fridge. You can see why he only served it after strenuous exercise, and even then he would pronounce that our wolfing down of the fried potatoes was driven by a 'false appetite', brought on by too much oxygen. The technique is all his, though. Frying pan on high heat, he melted a substantial piece of lard, which he would add to during the cooking with a few more spoonsful. Then he flung in the potatoes, half-crushed in his hands, and continued to turn, beat and chop them until he had a very rough mash that was flecked all through with crisp, fried shards. Even then he would carry on cooking it a little more; I think just to drive us crazy. Since I first sheepishly tried to recreate it with less life-threatening ingredients, I have found it to be a very useful part of many dishes, and it is very popular with tired staff late at night after the kitchen equivalent of cowboys and Indians.

Summer

gooseberries	strawberries
cherries	raspberries
apricots	peas and beans
kale	watermelon
chard	peaches
courgettes	melon
squash	tomatoes
beetroot	peppers

Gooseberry fool with gingered sponge fingers

The first and most important thing to say here is that you don't have to top and tail the gooseberries. That delicate and tedious operation must be the biggest reason for the relative unpopularity of berries in general, though I'm sure their sour taste has more relevance in the case of gooseberries. It's difficult to give specific quantities; so much depends on how strong you like your fool, so the basic instruction must be to make a syrup of the gooseberries and sugar, a light mousse of the cream, and to fold as much gooseberry into the cream as you see fit, to your own taste.

Fool is, surprisingly, one of the most popular lunch desserts in Café Paradiso, whether it be made from sour berries, rhubarb or sweet fruit like apricots.

FOR FOUR:

1kg gooseberries
500g sugar
500mls cream

2 eggs, separated
50g caster sugar
50g plain flour
20g cornflour
half teaspoon ground ginger
icing sugar, to serve

Put the gooseberries in a pan with the sugar and a tablespoon of water. Bring it very slowly to a boil and simmer very gently, stirring occasionally, until the fruit is very soft. Blend the fruit in a food processor, pass the purée through a sieve and leave it to cool.

Whisk the cream to soft peaks and fold in the gooseberry purée to your taste. Save a little of the purée to swirl on to the top of individual portions. You can serve the fool now or chill it again for up to a few hours before serving.

To make the sponge fingers, whisk the egg whites until stiff, then add half the caster sugar and whisk again for a minute. In another bowl, whisk the egg yolks and the rest of the caster sugar until pale and fluffy. Sift the flours and ginger together and fold into the egg yolks. Then fold in the egg whites. Use a piping bag to pipe lengths of the batter, 10cm by 2cm, on to baking trays lined with parchment. Bake at 180°C/350°F for 25 to 30 minutes, until pale golden. Leave to cool on the trays. Dredge the fingers with icing sugar before serving.

Cherries in kirsch with chocolate-olive oil mousse

Cherries have such a short season they are hardly on the menu before they disappear again. But that's okay because cherries are the first of the luscious summer fruits and their passing is only a sign that the rest are on their way: the strawberries, raspberries, peaches and currants. It could be said of most summer fruits that the nicest thing to do with them is to eat them on the way home from the shop, or on the way back up the garden path if you are so lucky as to have your own, and cherries are definitely in this category. Buy more than you intend to serve or you won't have enough for dinner. In Paradiso we make little tartlets packed with cherries, and cheesecakes too, but sometimes we serve them very simply, maybe doused in an alcoholic syrup, as here.

This recipe is equally an excuse to give you the chocolate mousse with olive oil. If it didn't show up here with the cherries, it would have later with raspberries, or even later with poached pears in the winter. It is an extraordinary mousse with a slightly chewy texture, almost-but-not-quite-nougat, which holds a lot of air bubbles, yet melts divinely in the mouth. I came across this recipe by Gabriela Llamas, a Spaniard, in the New Zealand magazine *Cuisine*, but I lost the magazine and the first year we made the mousse by guessing. It was all right, but nothing earth-shattering, and we persisted more for the novelty value than anything else. Then the magazine popped up from whatever misfiling system it had become lost in, we tried out the proper recipe and were blown away. Now, I envy anyone trying it for the first time. Use a good-quality chocolate with at least 70 per cent cocoa solids, and a fruity, nutty olive oil.

FOR FOUR:

150g dark chocolate
140mls olive oil
4 eggs, separated
125g caster sugar
1 tablespoon Cointreau or other orange liqueur
pinch salt

200g sugar
200mls water
50mls kirsch
400g fresh cherries

In a bowl over a pan of simmering water, melt the chocolate and slowly stir in the olive oil. Beat the egg yolks with half the sugar until pale and fluffy. Stir in the chocolate oil mix and the Cointreau. Whisk the egg whites with a pinch of salt until stiff, then continue whisking while adding the remaining sugar gradually in small batches. Fold the egg white mix into the chocolate and put the mousse into a fridge to chill for at least four hours. It has a strong structure, and should easily keep overnight.

Place the sugar, water and kirsch in a small pan and simmer for five minutes. Leave this syrup to cool to room temperature. It should be slightly thickened, just enough to coat the back of a spoon.

Leave the cherries whole and their stalks attached. When ready to serve, dunk the cherries in the syrup, put them on serving plates and pour a little more syrup over. Serve with a generous scoop of the mousse.

Vanilla-poached apricots with lemon and almond polenta cake and yoghurt

We rarely get Irish apricots, though I'm sure there are some optimists growing them here. However, imported apricots do show up for a brief time in June, and though it's easy to miss them, even to dismiss them as poor cousins of the peach and nectarine, they have their own charms, not least of which is the delightful way they give up their stones – anyone who has ever wrestled with a stubborn but ripe peach, trying to use a combination of gentleness, quickness and force while the flesh turned to mush and the juices ran off your elbows, will appreciate apricots. Vanilla goes very well with their rich sweetness, though very light touches of cinnamon or sweet ginger are good too.

The very lemony cake is a perfect foil for the sweet, poached apricots. Use a 24 x 34cm tin for the lemon cake, the shallow one often known as a Swiss roll tray. The quantity of cake mixture might appear to be a bit mean, but it will cook to a thickness of about 2cm, which is thin enough for the lemon syrup to penetrate almost to the bottom.

Because I think of this as an eastern Mediterranean dish, I would serve it with thick yoghurt rather than cream.

FOR FOUR:

200g butter
200g caster sugar
rind and juice of 3 lemons
3 eggs
100g plain flour
100g fine maize meal
50g ground almonds
1 teaspoon baking powder

100g light muscovado sugar

1 vanilla pod
150g sugar
8 apricots

Heat an oven to 180°C/350°F, and line your tin.

Melt the butter and caster sugar, and stir in the rind of one lemon. Whisk the eggs briefly, then whisk the butter/sugar mix into the eggs. Sift the flour, maize, almonds and baking powder together, then fold this into the batter. Pour this into the tin and bake it in the oven for 30 minutes. When the cake is done, prick it all over with a fork. Warm the muscovado sugar with the lemon juice and the rind of two lemons, then pour this all over the cake. Leave to cool to room temperature before eating.

Split the vanilla pod lengthways and scrape the inner seeds into a pan with the 150g of sugar, the vanilla pod and 250mls of water. Bring this slowly to a boil, while you halve the apricots and remove their stones. When the syrup boils, turn it down to a very low simmer and drop in the apricot halves. Cover the pan and simmer very gently for five minutes, maybe a few more, checking occasionally. Take the pan off the heat shortly before the apricots are fully cooked, remove the lid and leave the apricots to cool in their syrup. Serve the apricots warm or at room temperature over a slice of lemon cake, with a dollop of thick yoghurt.

Black kale with plum tomatoes, olive oil, garlic and chillies

My first and only source of black kale was, and still is, from Hollyhill Farm in West Cork, which grows vegetables for Café Paradiso. They have always grown it both outdoors and in tunnels, and have often managed to keep up a skeleton supply through ten or eleven months of the year. I love the vegetable too much to complain, though I did moan a bit last year when they only managed six months. I believe it is more naturally a winter vegetable but, over the years, I have come to welcome it most in early summer. Basically, I take it when I can get it, and I would advise anybody who comes across it to do the same.

This vegetable might be better, or even more properly, known as 'cavolo nero' or 'Tuscan cabbage'. 'Black kale' has been the functional name we use in Café Paradiso when identifying it to each other, the customers and even the growers. After a few initial phone conversations in the early days where it was identified as 'you know, that cavolo nero stuff, the black kale-type thing, the big stalky cabbage down the back of the tunnel', we fell into the habit of saying only 'black kale'. If a name is a form of identity, then it is well named. The plant grows as a stalk of two or three feet and puts out long leaves of the most extraordinarily beautiful green, so green it is almost black in a deep-blue-purple kind of way. If you could buy cloth of this shade, I would fill my wardrobe with it and wear nothing else. The leaves can be picked and the plant will go on producing more. The leaves can be pulled from their stems very easily; indeed it is a very satisfying chore. For all its beauty and generosity of production, it is the flavour of black kale that makes it by far my favourite green leaf vegetable. At once strong, earthy and sweet, the kale also seems to become rich and juicy when cooked, especially cooked in olive oil. It is still frustratingly rare commercially. Despite the elitist pleasure of having someone grow it exclusively for us in Paradiso, I would love it to be grown and cooked more widely.

This simple recipe contains what is just about my favourite food flavour combination. It is a slight variation on the basic model of green leaves wilted in olive oil. Strong, potentially bitter greens, cooked just right and long enough so they come up sweet and luscious with the help of the fruity richness of a good olive oil and some ripe tomatoes, topped off by a solid hit of chilli. It is almost extraordinary that it is the flavour of the kale itself that shines through this. If you think I exaggerate, try biting off a piece of raw kale, or cabbage, to see what the raw material is. Bitter, isn't it? Check this against the divine balance of sweet, rich, green and hot that this recipe produces in five minutes and you have the magic of simple cooking. As you chew almost-melting black kale, its inherent sweetly rich but strong and earthy flavour pushes through the upfront flavours of chilli, garlic and olive oil, and when they have faded the sweet kale is the last to linger. Eat kale this way with anything – your finest rich dinner, your simplest supper, or a poached egg and toast.

FOR FOUR:

200g black kale
4 plum tomatoes
2–4 cloves garlic
1–2 fresh red chillies
olive oil
a little stock and salt

Pull the leaves of kale off the stalks and tear them coarsely. Slice the tomatoes into thin wedges. Slice the garlic, but don't chop it finely. Check the heat of the chillies by nicking off a little bit and tasting it, decide how much chilli to use and whether to leave the seeds in or out, then slice them in half lengthways and chop the lengths into thin slices crossways.

Heat a couple of tablespoons of olive oil to quite hot in a pan and drop in the kale. Use tongs to toss the kale in the oil and keep it from burning. Add a splash of water or stock after a minute to add a touch of steam to the cooking. I would add a little salt now too.

The kale will wilt and take on a glossy sheen very quickly, and as soon as it does add the tomatoes, garlic and chillies. Keep tossing and stirring over a high heat, occasionally adding splashes of stock or water when the pan seems too dry, though the juice from the tomatoes will help here. Four or five minutes' cooking should do it. Pick out a little piece of kale to test. It will be softly chewy, sweet and oily when it's done… and perfectly warmly spiced if you got your guess right on the chillies. Check for seasoning and add a little salt, if needed.

Fresh pappardelle in sage butter with black kale, broad beans, artichokes and green peppercorns

Nine times out of ten, I would cook black kale as in the previous recipe, wilted in olive oil with or without the tomatoes and spices. Then it is a perfect side dish or can be stirred into pasta, risotto, pancakes and so on, and I could write a dozen recipes based on that prototype. Here is one recipe cut from a different cloth, where the kale is flavoured with sage butter.

Pappardelle is a very wide strand of pasta, 2–3cm, though it is often cut to less than half the length of, say, tagliatelle to compensate for the width. I use it for this recipe because I like the way the wide acreage of the pasta holds a rich coating of the sage butter. It's not an easily available cut of pasta, and even my local pasta supplier no longer makes it. Her new machine is too clever and pleased with its efficiency to take pappardelle on board. Chances are that the pasta roller in the back of your cupboard doesn't have a wide enough blade either. Never mind. When I want to use pappardelle, I either make my own pasta or buy a length of fresh pasta sheet from a good shop, and cut it myself with a knife. To do this using fresh local or homemade pasta, first cut pieces of pasta about 18 to 20cm long. Roll each length up loosely and slice them into strips about 1 to 1.5cm wide – bearing in mind that the strands will almost double in width when boiled. A slightly jagged and uneven cut of the pasta is a characteristic that will impress your friends, whether or not you've admitted that you didn't actually make the pasta. If you do make your own, cut the final strands by hand, without too much fuss, to give the pasta a lovely handmade quality. It's surely a golden rule that, if you go to a whole lot of trouble preparing dinner, the food shouldn't look like you bought it from a chilled food shelf on the way home from the office.

It is a rare day when I use butter or cream with pasta in the summer. Usually it's olive oil every time in our house, from the first of the glorious Irish summer down-pours to the last. But when I first put this combination together a few years ago it was a big hit, so I've left well alone. The black kale and the pasta become rich and luscious with absorbed sage butter, and the cracked green peppercorns add a lovely warm kick. I love the combination in green peppercorns of heat and fragrance, and the light, hollow freeze-dried ones are my favourite.

Looking at the recipe now, however, it is obvious that it is a very adaptable one. The basic combination of pasta and sage butter will happily take on other greens throughout the year, and leeks and mushrooms love sage too.

Make the sage butter anything up to a few hours, or even days, before you need it, and make plenty. It keeps well for weeks in a sealed container in the fridge, and if you get to like it you will find yourself dousing lots of stuff with it – potatoes, pasta, eggs, steamed vegetables…

Pan-fried courgettes with cherry tomatoes, basil and garlic, on a new-potato tortilla

A lovely way to cook, and to present, 'baby' courgettes. I hesitate to use the phrase 'baby courgettes', because I don't really consider those little ones to be babies at all, but proper-sized courgettes. I tend to go along with the definition of a courgette I first read in Digby Law's *Vegetable Book*. The courgettes should be picked and eaten when no bigger than your little finger, while the flesh is still sweet and fairly concentrated, and before they have developed bitter seeds and taken on too much water to taste of anything.

The annual glut of courgettes is one of the banes of my life – a lot I've got to worry about, eh? – and one of the few things about summer that makes my heart sink. Because the plant is so productive, too many people grow too many courgette plants as a cash crop, selling the swollen marrow by the kilogram, thereby transferring from the kitchen to the garden that old cynical catering ambition to find ways to sell water. Mostly, I avoid courgettes completely except for the crops grown locally for Café Paradiso by people who will agree to pick small ones for me. We stuff the flowers, with or without little courgettes attached, and we cook courgettes either whole or halved, in recipes like this one where the vegetables are cooked briefly with their favourite summer partners of olive oil, garlic, tomatoes and basil. The courgettes themselves are never more than a day or two old and never much bigger than, well, let's say my biggest finger. Even so, the crop is still huge. At first, I used the carrot of higher prices to persuade growers to pick the courgettes early. Now, they prefer them that way, and they are beginning to think that the plant still produces close to the same amount of vegetable by weight as it would if left to grow monster marrows. They still like the higher prices, though.

This dish is one of those that came about from trying to make a special dinner from very fresh seasonal vegetables, and realising that no amount of twisting, wrapping, stuffing, layering or anything else would do the vegetables as much justice as cooking them briefly with ingredients they love to be with. Here, the courgettes, cooked in a simple way that might often relegate them to a side-dish role, are served on an individual new potato and egg tortilla, which might properly be the focus of the dish. In a sense, the dish is inverted, or at least the focus is shifted to bring the courgettes into the limelight. The tortilla differs from traditional tortilla in that it contains boiled waxy new potato slices set in the egg rather than chipped and fried floury potatoes, and it tastes lighter and more summery for it. Don't try to please Spanish guests with it though; they may doubt your grasp on the basics of life.

Of course you can cook one big tortilla to fill a frying pan and cut wedges from it, and it will taste good, but I think these individual ones suit new potatoes and the composed, elegant look you are aiming for in the finished dish.
If you do cook this, or indeed any courgette dish, with big, fat truncheon-like marrows, slice them in half lengthways and scrape out the seeds before slicing the flesh. But, first, let your vegetable supplier know you're a bit grumpy about having to work with such monsters. Oh, and agree to pay more for proper, smaller, courgettes.

FOR FOUR:

400g small waxy new potatoes

6 eggs

4 spring onions, sliced thinly

salt and pepper, to season

600g courgettes

1 small red onion

6 cloves garlic

200g cherry tomatoes

olive oil, to brush pan and rings

2 tablespoons olive oil

large pinch salt and pepper

splash of stock or water

1 handful basil leaves

Cut the potatoes into half moons of half to 1cm thick and cook them in boiling water until just tender. Beat the eggs well and stir in the potato, spring onion, and plenty of salt and pepper.

Slice the courgettes in half lengthways, or leave very small ones whole. Quarter the red onions and slice them thinly. Slice the garlic cloves quite thin. Halve the cherry tomatoes. Place four steel rings of 8–10cm diameter, 2cm high, in a wide frying pan. Put the pan over a low, wide flame and brush the pan and the sides of the rings with olive oil. After a few minutes, fill each ring with the egg and potato mixture. Leave the tortillas to cook for at least five minutes before flipping them over quickly. Tap down the sides of the rings to prevent too much egg leakage – the egg will set very quickly anyway, so there should-n't be much spillage, even if your flipping is not up to speed. Let the tortillas continue cooking over a low heat. Turn them once or twice more to check the cooking side, and press the tops gently to test their firmness. If the tortillas are cooked before the courgettes, turn the heat off and leave them in the pan, or keep them in a low oven.

While the tortillas are cooking, heat two tablespoons of olive oil to a fairly high heat in a wide pan and toss in the courgettes. Cook for two minutes, stirring and tossing, then add the red onion and garlic, and continue cooking for one minute more, reducing the heat to avoid burning the garlic. Add a splash of stock or water to help prevent this. Now add the cherry tomatoes and a large pinch of salt and pepper. With the heat on medium, cook for one minute more until the tomatoes just begin to soften. Tear the basil leaves and stir them in, adding a splash each of olive oil and stock or water. These will combine with the tomatoes to form a lovely juice.

Place the tortillas – cut in half if you like – on plates, and pile a generous mound of courgettes over each, pouring every last drop of juice from the pan over the vegetables.

Roast beetroot with balsamic vinegar, caraway and wilted greens

Although I try to use beetroots for as much of the year as I can get them – in any variety or size, and changing the dishes for the large stored roots of winter – my true love is the first crop of tiny, rock-hard beets freshly pulled from the warm ground in summer. And, as with most vegetables whose annual arrival is anxiously awaited, the first thing I do with it is cook it my favourite way. In beetroot's case, that's roasted in olive oil until the beets begin to caramelise on the outside, then finished with a dash of balsamic vinegar for a few minutes more roasting. I serve these beets to anyone who will have them, to complement all kinds of food but especially rich dishes like risotto, crêpes, baked goats' cheese or feta dishes, and so on.

However, the first time I put caraway seeds with roasted beets was to serve with some Moroccan-spiced spring rolls – I don't know if caraway is particularly Moroccan, and I doubt that beetroot is, but the combination had an exotic flavour that was exactly what I was looking for. I don't think caraway gets much attention in modern cooking, but maybe it never did. The only way I remember caraway being used in the food of my childhood was in the caraway bread made by a local bakery at Christmas – a slightly sweetened and enriched yeast bread eaten in thick slabs with butter. It was my grandfather's official and often-declared favourite food: he would look forward to it for weeks, and devour it for the few days it was available. Now it puzzles me that neither he nor anyone else questioned its short seasonal appearance, or begged the bakery, which was two doors from his home, to make it more often. Anyway, if caraway isn't your favourite spice, the more popular cumin is a lovely replacement.

If the beets come with young leaves attached, use these as part or all of the greens in the recipe. If you are not using the beets immediately, chop off the greens and store them separately, as the greens will draw moisture from the root, causing the roots to dry out and soften sooner. But I bet you knew that already.

FOR FOUR:

20 small beetroots
olive oil
salt
1 tablespoon balsamic vinegar
1 teaspoon caraway seeds
1 red onion, thinly sliced
4 large handfuls greens, such as beet, chard or spinach
salt and pepper, to season

Trim the greens from the beets, leaving just a centimetre at the top of the roots, and leave any tail on for now. Cook the beets in boiling water for 30 minutes or so, then lift the beets out to a bowl of cold water. Rub the skins of the beets while in the cold water or, better still, under running water. The skins and the tail will slip off easily.

Put the beets in an oven dish, splash on a tablespoon of olive oil and some salt, and toss the beets to coat them. Cook the beets in a fairly hot oven, about 190°C/375°F, until beginning to crinkle and caramelise, about 15 minutes. Shake the dish now and again to ensure even cooking. Now sprinkle on the balsamic vinegar and the caraway seeds and return the dish to the oven for a further five minutes.

Heat two tablespoons of olive oil in a large pan and toss in the greens and onion slices. Stir the greens with tongs until they shrink and take on a glossy look, adding a splash of water if they seem too dry or inclined to burn. Season well with salt and pepper.

Lift the greens on to a serving dish and place the beets on and around them

Beetroot with spices in a coconut-rice flour pancake with a scallion and pistachio cream

This dish is based on a beetroot curry I ate as part of a wonderful feast we had one evening in Rasa, the extraordinary vegetarian Indian restaurant in London. We also had a garlic curry but I haven't thought of anything to do with that yet! Here I have put a version of the curry into a coconut and rice flour pancake, which I use for many dishes. The pancakes are not as flexible as crêpes, which is why I cook them just before serving, when they are most pliable. They do keep for a few days and reheat well, but might not fold so easily. The curry has such a beautiful colour that I only partly cover it with the pancake. You could serve some rice and maybe one or two other curries with the pancake, or make it part of a series of individual courses. I think it's too good-looking to be dumping other curries on the plate.

The recipe includes a quantity of fresh coconut. Do try to use fresh if you can get it but, if not, desiccated will do. To get the flesh from a coconut, break the nut with a hammer and pull the hard shell off the white flesh. Grate the flesh with a wide grater.

The scallion cream was an idea I took from the book *Charlie Trotter's Vegetables*, an incredible and stunningly beautiful volume, full of the most outlandish things to do with, or to, vegetables. Any of you who know Trotter's books, or his food if you're lucky, will be familiar with the constant sense of 'How does he do that?' or even 'What kind of a mind even started down that path… with potatoes and peas?' Well, there I was one evening, flicking through the book looking for inspiration, when my eye fell on one of the many beautiful green oils, sauces and emulsions in the photographs. I checked the recipe and then had my first Charlie Trotter 'I could do that!' moment: it was ecstatic, I can tell you. I added the pistachios and cardamom to give it an eastern twist and a little cream to enrich the sauce.

Strawberries with balsamic vinegar and Thai basil

As sweet as strawberries are, a spoonful of sugar does wonderful things for them…
but vinegar? A regular smartarse order in Café Paradiso is 'the balsamic strawberries
without the balsamic'. That's strawberries, sugar and cream, then, sir, just like
mummy used to make? Actually, my own mother was one of the first to try to get
away with the 'hold the balsamic' line, but I wouldn't budge. Afterwards, she said it
was 'quite nice, unusual, but not as nice as strawberries without balsamic vinegar'! It
is a bit of a cheffy concoction but, no, I didn't invent it – it goes back at least as far
as nouvelle cuisine, and may well have an authentic Italian pedigree, for all I know.
You do need a very good balsamic vinegar, however, one with a rich, intense and
rounded flavour, with natural concentrated sweetness as well as the acidity of
vinegar. It should be traditionally aged for at least six years, though ten years and
older is better for sweet dishes. Cheap balsamic is no better than general red wine
vinegar and will only make your strawberries sour.

The basil element of the dish is not my idea either. John Foley, the book designer,
called me one morning to say, among other more urgent things, that he had made a
fantastic discovery the previous night while rummaging in his fridge for dinner…
strawberries and basil. I briefly fantasised about what other combinations he had
pondered and rejected before settling on that, but said nothing and carefully filed
the information on a scrap of paper from my back pocket. Then when our organic
strawberries came on stream, I tried this version, which combines John's with the
balsamic strawberries I had been toying with; mostly, I admit, for the fun value of
pairing such 'savoury' flavourings with everybody's favourite summer fruit. I was
pleased that it worked, but I was surprised at just how well. Yum, that's delicious. I
tried a number of different basils because I had the luxury of having visited the
gardens of Ballymaloe Cookery School a few days earlier and had been sent home
with 10 of their 20-something varieties. This 'Thai basil' was my favourite with
strawberries; it has a quite pronounced aniseed flavour and hints of mint over a
fairly mellow layer of classic basil taste. Most basils will work, though some that I
tried were overpowering – avoid the fashionable dark purple ones, which are very
strong and a little bitter. Having enjoyed the variety of basils at Ballymaloe, I'm
going to grow a few of my own in a pot, though not 20! I suggest you do the same.

FOR FOUR:

2 punnets strawberries
1 tablespoon balsamic
vinegar
4 tablespoons sugar
10 small leaves Thai basil

Slice any large strawberries in half and leave
the rest whole. Toss the strawberries in a
bowl with the balsamic vinegar and sugar,
and leave them for 10–20 minutes. This will
draw out the sweet juices of the strawberries
to form a thin syrup with the balsamic and
sugar, but any longer and the strawberries
may start to become a little mushy. Just
before you serve, tear the basil leaves and stir
them gently into the strawberries.

Roasted green beans and shallots with couscous and marinated feta

The key to avoiding this pilaf becoming a stodgy and dull dish is to see it as a vegetable dish more than a couscous one – a big pile of sweet, roasted beans and shallots wrapped in a flavoursome blend of herbs, citrus and chilli, all bound together by the starchy, puffed-up granules of couscous. Marinated feta adds a richness that I can't resist putting in, though you may well find that the pilaf is perfect without the cheese. Cooking beans this way, by oven roasting, is best suited to the rougher element in the bean family. Delicate fine beans will end up all charred skin with no inner sweetness. You need runner beans, flat beans, the long, wide and substantial ones. Shallots are a bit of a chore, but worth it sometimes for their lovely caramelised sweetness. Small red onions or baby leeks, sliced, would be the next best thing.

Marinating feta gives it an extra dimension. In a few hours, the marinade doesn't penetrate far into the cheese; it's more like putting a coat of warm, fragrant spice over the cheese's body of salty creaminess. I use a simple marinade of garlic, chilli and rosemary in olive oil. Use a generous amount of olive oil in the marinade; it won't go to waste, as the oil also takes on the flavours of the marinade; and even some of the feta's saltiness. Drizzle some of it over the finished pilaf, and keep the rest to drizzle over tomorrow's dinner or to make a salad dressing.

You can use this pilaf as a simple main course, and it also makes a lovely warm salad, either as a starter or as part of an outdoor picnic or barbecue. Or you can take it as a basic model and add other vegetables, both roasted and steamed.

FOR FOUR:

200g feta cheese
4 cloves garlic
2–4 hot chillies, halved
a few sprigs thyme or rosemary
olive oil

20 small shallots
300g couscous
1 teaspoon turmeric
rind of 1 orange, finely grated
rind of 1 lime, finely grated
salt and pepper, to season
500g green beans
4 cloves garlic, sliced
2 fresh red chillies
1 tablespoon cumin seeds
1 tablespoon fennel seeds
splash of stock or water
4 tablespoons cooked chickpeas
small handful mint leaves, torn roughly
small handful fresh coriander, chopped
1 lime

Marinate the feta at least an hour before you want to serve the couscous. Chop the feta into rough cubes of about 15mm. Put the pieces in a bowl with the whole garlic cloves, chillies and the rosemary or thyme sprigs. Pour in enough olive oil to cover the cheese. Peel the shallots, toss them in a little olive oil in an oven dish and roast them at about 160°C/325°F until they have softened a little and are beginning to colour.

While the shallots are cooking, soak the couscous. Stir the turmeric, orange and lime rind into the dry couscous, season with salt and pepper and pour in 300mls of hot, not boiling, water. Stir the couscous once and leave it to soak until the vegetables are cooked.

Slice the green beans diagonally into pieces of about 5cm, add these and the garlic to the shallots. Toss well to coat everything in oil, turn the heat up to 190°C/375°F and put the dish back in the oven. Cook for five minutes, then slice the chillies into rings and add them, along with the cumin and fennel seeds.

Add a splash of stock or water to keep the beans from burning, and cook for a few minutes more until the beans are browning a little and just tender. Stir in the chickpeas, mint and coriander. Sift the couscous with a fork or your fingers and stir it into the vegetables. If you want to serve the dish hot, rather than warm, return the entire dish to the oven for a few minutes. Otherwise serve it as it is now – I think this kind of food is good at just above room temperature, probably better. Spoon the vegetables on to plates, scatter some cubes of feta around each and drizzle some of the oil from the feta marinade around and over the vegetables. Finish by squeezing some lime juice over the vegetables.

Oven-roasted peaches with lavender and honey ice cream and pistachio biscotti

The truism that the best thing to do with perfectly ripe fruit is to eat it from the tree must surely apply to the peach more than any other. The combination of the rich, sweet flavour and the uncontrollable juices streaming down your chin and elbows can cause you to wolf down the peach in a sensuous frenzy that leaves you a little shocked afterwards as you suck the last of the flavour from the stone, looking for somewhere polite to put it. Unfortunately, it is also true that, as the peach has become more commonplace, the perfectly ripe peach is becoming more elusive. How often do you buy peaches at the supermarket and find them disappointing in a ho-hum ordinary kind of way; or, worse still, you eat one without noticing, mindlessly reading a newspaper. A peach as ordinary, humdrum mild disappointment is a travesty. It could be seen as a symbol of the marketing of food as dull, safe, acceptable but cheap and ever-present, which should shock us into anger and disgust. Mostly we carry on reading the paper and gradually forget what a peach tastes like. In Paradiso we have a wonderful supply of organic peaches from France, which I wait for, in prayer, each summer before using this recipe, or indeed any peach recipe. I recently demonstrated this dish to a group of enthusiastic food lovers, a large number of whom said they had never tasted such wonderful peaches; and they didn't mean the way they were cooked. As much as I like people to appreciate my cooking, I get a bigger kick when they fall in love with the ingredients.

Peaches are a gift from the gods or one of the greatest pleasures of nature, depending on which way your beliefs lean. Do take the trouble to search out good ones, pay whatever is asked and, above all, reject common, cheap imitations.

Check peaches by smell first and then texture, rather than colour. Ripe, good-quality peaches will give off a rich fragrance and will be heavy and firm but not hard. Though they should have no green skin, a lot of red skin doesn't mean the peach is either ripe or tasty, as they are often bred and modified to turn red easily and quickly.

In fact, what strikes people about this dish, often more than the peaches, is the lavender ice cream, an idea that Bridget brought back from a trip home to New Zealand. Lavender flowers bloom just in time for the peach season, making this a perfect match. The number of lavender flowers given here makes a sublimely flavoured ice cream; don't be tempted to go for a bigger flavour as I was the second time I tried it, or you'll end up throwing out an ice cream that tastes like soap. Also, not all lavenders are good in food; the one we use is known as English lavender, or sometimes French lavender. The one I use has an inch-long head of tight purple pods.

FOR FOUR:

FOR THE ICE CREAM:
350mls milk
6 heads lavender flowers
5 egg yolks
100g sugar
1 tablespoon honey
300mls cream

Bring the milk to a boil and drop in the lavender flower heads. Simmer very gently for two minutes, then remove from the heat and leave for 30 minutes.

Whisk together the egg yolks, sugar and honey until pale and creamy. Strain the milk into the egg mix, then heat this custard gently, stirring all the time, until it has thickened slightly. Cool the custard completely, then stir in the cream. Freeze the ice cream custard using an ice cream machine.

FOR THE BISCOTTI:
200g plain flour
200g caster sugar
2 teaspoons baking powder
2 eggs, lightly beaten
rind of 1 lemon
40g sultanas
40g dried apricots, sliced
40g dates
80g shelled pistachios
40g hazelnuts

Mix flour, sugar and baking powder together in a food mixer. Add half of the egg and mix well. Add the remaining egg and beat well to get a soft, slightly sticky dough. Now add the lemon rind, dried fruit and nuts, and mix everything well.

Weigh the dough and divide into it into four. Roll each quarter into a long tubular shape of about 3–4cm diameter. Place these tubes well apart on parchment-lined oven trays, and bake at 180°C/350°F for 30–40 minutes until pale golden. Remove from the oven and cool for 15 minutes. Turn the oven down to 140°C/275°F. Slice the cooled biscotti dough across at an angle into slices of about 10mm thick. Lay the slices on the baking sheets and bake them again for ten minutes, then turn the slices over and bake for ten more minutes. The biscotti will still be slightly soft, but will become crisp very quickly as they cool. They will keep for weeks in a sealed jar or tin.

TO SERVE:
6–8 peaches
4 tablespoons clarified butter (see page 58)
1 tablespoon honey

Halve the peaches, remove the stones, and place the fruit in an oven dish. Melt the clarified butter and stir in the honey. Spoon the honey-flavoured butter over the peaches and roast them under a grill, on a barbecue or in a hot oven. Serve the peaches warm with ice cream and biscotti.

Charentais melon sorbet with honey and rosewater baklava

Having been brought up with the notion that melon was some icily cold, tasteless thing you got as a starter for Sunday lunch in country hotels, even in the dead of winter, I am wary of melons in general – a wariness that has become subconscious and that I have to struggle with every summer. Those hotel starters were almost always made from the variety called 'honeydew', though they could have been called anything for all the flavour they carried. Nowadays, there are two varieties of melon that I work with, though I know I should try harder to expand that repertoire… but the memories begin to surface and I turn away. Watermelons I have come to love, as much for their thirst-quenching qualities and their dramatic size and colour as anything else. Watermelon may be the flashiest of melons, and the most satisfying to scoff from the fridge on a scorching afternoon, but the charentais, or cantaloupe, is far and away the king when it comes to flavour. Rich, sweet and fragrant, it has a dense, orange flesh and a beautiful scent – a good, perfectly ripe cantaloupe will call to you with its fragrant perfume as you pass it in the market.

You definitely need a well-flavoured melon to make into sorbet, as there is some dilution of flavour in the process. Here we serve the melon sorbet with baklava, but it is great on its own or with a salad of fresh melons.

The baklava recipe is essentially the classic version of pastry and nuts baked in as many layers as you can make, then drenched with a very sweet honey and rosewater syrup, which not only gives the baklava most of its flavour but helps it to keep fresh and crisp for a long time. I know this because one evening a woman told a waitress in Paradiso that the baklava was dry and tasteless; luckily I checked before taking a stand in defence of my baklava; we had been selling all evening a baklava made without syrup. It was worse than dry and tasteless, she was being polite. No one was seriously injured in the fallout in the kitchen.

FOR FOUR:

FOR THE SORBET:
200g sugar
200mls water
1 medium charentais melon
2 tablespoons lemon juice
2 egg whites

Make a sugar syrup by putting the sugar and 200mls water in a pan, bringing it to a boil and simmering for one minute. Leave the syrup to cool.

Peel the melon and blend the flesh with the lemon juice in a food processor, then pass this purée through a sieve. Beat the egg whites briefly with a fork to froth them a little, then stir this into the melon purée with 350mls of the sugar syrup. Freeze, using an ice cream machine.

FOR THE BAKLAVA:
400g whole almonds
50g light muscovado sugar
half teaspoon ground cinnamon
half teaspoon ground ginger
1 packet filo pastry
225g unsalted butter, melted
100g caster sugar
125g honey
1 and a half tablespoons rosewater

You need a 24 x 30cm oven dish, which will give 16 portions: 32 triangular pieces. Lightly toast the almonds, then chop them finely and mix them with the muscovado sugar, cinnamon and ginger.

Cut the filo pastry to fit the dish, saving any cut-off pieces to make up layers in the middle of the procedure. Brush the dish with butter, lay a sheet of pastry in it, brush that with butter, cover it with another sheet and brush that also with butter. Scatter on a layer of the almonds, then put two more layers of pastry as before. Continue in this way until the almonds and pastry are all used up. Make sure the almonds are scattered evenly to the edges so that the dish is building up evenly. Brush the top pastry sheet with butter and chill the dish for 30 minutes. Heat the oven to 190°c/375°F, with the fan turned off if you have one.

Using a sharp knife, cut the baklava into 16 rectangles, four by four, then cut each one in half diagonally to get 32 triangles. Make sure you cut right to the base of the dish. Bake the baklava for ten minutes, then turn the oven down to 160°c/325°F for an hour. The baklava should be lightly browned on top and crisp all the way through.

Heat the caster sugar, honey and rosewater together in a small pan until bubbling, leave it for one minute, then pour it over the hot baklava. Leave the baklava in the dish to cool completely before removing the pieces. It will keep for a week or more in a sealed container.

Buffalo mozzarella with organic tomato salad and a warm olive-basil dressing

The tomato has become such a staple of modern food that it would be hard to get through a day without meeting one. The world, or at least the parts of it we live in, takes the tomato completely for granted. Tomatoes are available every day of the year in every cornershop and supermarket, fresh and tinned, puréed and juiced. In the ketchups, sauces, chutneys, frozen foods and so on of our pantries, the tomato is a fundamental ingredient. In Paradiso, as everywhere, tomatoes are used in many ways in so many dishes, all through the year. Even in winter, we use dried tomatoes, roasted tomatoes, frozen tomato sauces and tinned tomatoes. During the times of year when we can get good fresh tomatoes, they still mostly tend to play either supporting or partial roles in dishes, or act as the base for sauces, stews and relishes. But in late summer, when tomatoes are at their prime, I serve them raw with olive oil, salt and pepper. This is the time to remind ourselves what a tomato tastes like. Because despite the tons of tomatoes we all get through during the year, we rarely stop to pay them much attention. So, when the time and the tomatoes are right, I like to present a plate of perfectly ripe, organic tomatoes, three or more varieties grown for their flavour rather than for their keeping qualities or crop yield, and ripened in their own good time in summer sunshine. In the right atmosphere, in the right frame of mind, everybody will notice the flavour and love it; most will be surprised. I enjoy those moments, seeing the look on a face, whether it is a first appreciation of a food or an unexpected flashback.

However if you write 'tomato salad' on a restaurant menu containing all sorts of other exotic attractions, then the reality is you're going to end up with a few boxes of over-ripe tomatoes at the end of the week and then it's tomato soup again all next week. So I usually serve the tomato salad with one or more eye-catching foods, something irresistible or of perceived high value. From a list including pesto-topped crostini, roasted sweetcorn, a herbed mousse, sheep's or goats' cheeses, shaved Parmesan, olives and anything including the word basil, my favourite is the classic combination of tomatoes with fresh buffalo mozzarella. Sometimes we dress the salad very simply with olive oil and salt; on other days we will concoct a slightly more complex dressing like the one in this recipe. But whatever we serve with them, we never lose sight of the fact that it is the tomatoes themselves that we want the diners to notice. This is the time to treat tomatoes as the extraordinary fruits that they are, the crown jewels of the most glorious time of the year.

If you don't have the simple luxury of your own tomatoes, take care to buy sun-ripened organic ones and try different varieties if you have the opportunity. Tomatoes taste better at room temperature, so avoid putting them in the fridge if you are going to eat them soon.

FOR FOUR:

2 x 200g pieces buffalo mozzarella

600–800g tomatoes

salt and black pepper, to season

10 kalamata olives, stoned and chopped into fine dice

150mls oil, 1 bunch basil

Tear the mozzarella pieces in half and put one half on each plate. Using a variety of tomatoes from tiny sweet cherry tomatoes through to the giant, dense fleshy ones. Slice or chop the tomatoes. Arrange the slices around the mozzarella and sprinkle some salt, coarsely ground black pepper and the finely chopped olives over both the tomatoes and the cheese. Blend the olive oil and basil and drizzle a generous stream of basil oil over everything and serve. To make a fabulous and substantial lunch of this starter, add some crusty bread or warm crostini, and take it out into the garden.

Tomato rasam

All summer long, and into the autumn, we make a roasted tomato soup in Café Paradiso, an almost shockingly intense concentration of tomatoes with garlic and summer herbs. The very simple recipe for that soup is in *The Café Paradiso Cookbook*, so this time around I thought I might give you a recipe for another, very different, tomato soup. I first came across rasam in the books of Das Sreedharan, two slightly different recipes in two books, which intrigued me, so I went looking for other versions of the dish. I found plenty, all different, some radically so, including one that claimed it to be the precursor of mulligatawny, that most English of Indian dishes. In the end I went back to Das's versions, because they were closest to what I had originally liked about the dish, that it was a thin invigorating broth rather than a soup, and I liked his description of it as a healing drink, a pick-me-up, a refreshing and cleansing tonic for any time of day. In Paradiso, we use our own ginger broth in the same way. The customers get it as part of a noodle dish but in the kitchen we drink it from cups to kick-start the evening. So the aim here was to make an Indian-spiced version. The main difference between my version and Das's is that I use only the broth from the lentils, not the lentils themselves, which gives a lighter finish, and I roast the tomatoes first to intensify their sweetness.

There is a chilli element in the spicing of the rasam, but it's not too upfront. Instead the broth is a soothing blend of the fruity sourness of tamarind, the sweetness of roasted tomatoes and the earthiness of the lentils. The dominant flavours are provided by the fragrant spices, which are barely cooked in oil and swirled into the broth at the last minute. If you were to make large batches of this to keep for days, I would recommend that you only fry sufficient spices as you intend to stir into each serving, as the lively freshness of recently introduced spices will fade to a more absorbed effect if left overnight. That's not a bad thing, merely different.

The broth is a first course, a light lunch or a cure, depending on your needs. It hasn't quite displaced the ginger broth in the Paradiso kitchen, but mostly because it is a little more complicated to make.

This recipe makes two litres, enough for eight to ten starters, but it's worth making at least that much, especially if you become fond enough of it to take a cupful as a refreshing drink.

FOR EIGHT TO TEN
STARTERS:

100g red lentils

1200mls vegetable stock
(see page 144)

1kg tomatoes, quartered

olive oil, to coat

salt, to season

8 cloves garlic

3cm x 4cm piece of
ginger, chopped

2 fresh green chillies,
chopped

2 teaspoons turmeric

small bunch fresh
coriander

150g tamarind pulp

3 tablespoons olive oil

1 teaspoon green
peppercorns, crushed

2 teaspoon mustard seeds

2 teaspoon fennel seeds

1 teaspoon cumin seeds

Wash the lentils and put them in a pot with the stock. Bring it to a boil and simmer over very low heat, covered, for 20 minutes. Take it off the heat and leave to cool.

Put the tomatoes in an oven dish with just enough olive oil to coat them, and some salt. Roast the tomatoes in a moderate oven for 15 minutes, until soft and juicy but only lightly coloured. Add the garlic and ginger for the last five minutes of the roasting. Take the tomatoes from the oven, stir in the chillies, the turmeric and the fresh coriander, then pour the tomatoes into a food processor and blend them to a fine purée.

Break up the tamarind and put it in a jug with 800mls of warm water to soak for ten minutes, then strain the liquid through a fine sieve, pushing the pulp with the back of a spoon to squeeze all the liquid through the sieve. Pass the lentils through the same sieve, without pushing, to save the broth and discard any of the lentil mush that doesn't pass through. Don't force it but don't fret about any solids that sneak through. Put the lentil broth, the tamarind juice and the tomato purée into a pot, bring it to a boil and simmer for 15 minutes.

In a frying pan, heat three tablespoons of olive oil and add the green peppercorns and the mustard, fennel and cumin seeds. Fry the spices for a few minutes until the mustard seeds begin to pop. Ladle the soup into bowls and swirl some of the spiced oil through each portion.

Tomato, saffron ricotta and olive tart

My love of tomato tarts would be more or less evenly split between those that are set by a custard, like the one below, and those that are little more than roasted tomatoes placed in pastry with some herbs. A tart without custard is a wonderful way to show off good tomatoes, but I think they work best as individual tarts, or as small ones at least – and, for some reason, I had it in mind to include a large tart recipe here. This tart, though of the custard variety, is crammed with tomatoes, so in some ways it's a compromise between the two styles. It's a very simple tart, as tomato dishes should be when tomatoes are at their best. Because the tomatoes retain a lot of their juiciness, the tart doesn't really need a sauce or relish, but I would sometimes serve it with a classic basil pesto.

The tart case is a basic shortcrust pastry. The pastry can be rolled and stored in the freezer any time in the days before you use it.

FOR FOUR:

160g plain flour
1 teaspoon salt
80g cold unsalted butter
40mls cold water

10 tomatoes, halved
salt and pepper, to season
drizzle olive oil
6 strands saffron
250g ricotta
4 eggs
100mls cream
50g Parmesan, finely grated
2 tablespoons tomato pesto (see page 30)
10g kalamata olives, stoned and sliced

Put the flour and salt into a food processor. Chop the butter into pieces, add it to the flour and process in short bursts until you get a fine crumb texture. Tip the mix into a bowl, pour in the water and bring the dough together with a few quick stirs with a spoon, then tip the dough out on to a lightly floured surface and knead it a few times to form a smooth ball. Press the ball gently to flatten it a little, wrap it tightly and refrigerate it for half an hour or more. Roll the pastry to fit a 26cm tart tin, preferably one with a loose base and with a 3–4cm-high side. Prick the pastry all over with a fork and refrigerate it again for at least half an hour, or until you need it. Before you use the pastry, blind-bake it in a medium oven until the pastry is just firm.

Place the tomatoes, cut side up, on an oven tray. Season with salt and pepper and drizzle over some olive oil. Roast the tomatoes in the oven at a medium temperature until softened and coloured a little. Soak the saffron threads in a tablespoon of hot water for a few minutes. Put the ricotta, eggs and cream, and the saffron and its water, into a food processor, and blend briefly to get a smooth custard. Season with salt and pepper. Stir in the grated Parmesan.

Spread a thin layer of the tomato pesto on to the base of the prepared pastry case, then pour in the custard. Scatter the sliced olives over it, then place the tomatoes, cut side up, into the custard. Press them in gently. Bake the tart at 180°C/350°F for 30 to 40 minutes, until the custard is set and lightly browned. Leave the tart for ten minutes before slicing it.

Summer stew of sweet peppers, new potatoes and sugar snaps with basil, garlic and olives, and goats' cheese ciabatta

A variation on the peperonata recipe from *The Café Paradiso Cookbook*. Here, the meltingly delicious olive oil-based pepper stew is given some added substance with some new potatoes, fresh waxy potatoes that don't break up or leak into the stew in the way you might want potatoes to do in a winter stew. And then, at the end of the slow cooking, I throw in a handful or two of crunchy sugar snaps, the vegetable that seems to best capture the essence of a fine, sunny summer. The stew is complete in itself, a lovely summer lunch, and needs only some crusty bread or, if you want something more elaborate, goats' cheese ciabatta. The recipe for the ciabatta doesn't have proper quantities – simply cover the bread with cheese. I like to scrape a thin layer of olive tapenade, preferably a green olive one, on to the bread under the cheese. Any pesto works very well too.

The flavour of the stew is a fairly upfront matter, in the sense that there aren't many background elements. There is a lot of garlic, but it remains in big pieces and cooks to a mellow sweetness. The peppers and garlic trade flavours with the olive oil, giving as well as taking, and that blending of flavours becomes the body of the stew. In such a blending the oil is more than a mere carrier, and its own flavour is very important. My favourite style of oil for this stew is a deep green one, very fruity but not really peppery or spicy. If you have some basil oil in the house, add a tablespoon or two of it with the tomatoes.

....

FOR FOUR:

FOR THE STEW:
2 small red onions
100mls olive oil
6–8 red and/or yellow peppers
1 fresh mild red chilli
10 cloves garlic, halved or sliced thickly
4 ripe tomatoes
12 black olives, stoned and halved
320g new potatoes
200g sugar snaps
1 bunch basil leaves
salt and black pepper, to season

Chop the red onions in half, then into thin slices. Heat the olive oil in a wide pan and start the onions cooking in it. Chop the peppers into quarters lengthways; scrape out the seeds and white membrane, and discard. Chop the pepper quarters into diagonal slices about 15mm thick. Slice the chilli in half lengthways and chop the halves into thin slices. Add the peppers, chilli and garlic to the onions in the pan, tossing well to coat everything in olive oil. Chop the tomatoes in half, slice them thickly and add them to the pan with the olives. When everything heats through again, cover the pan, turn the heat to the lowest setting and simmer the stew for 20 minutes.

Meanwhile, chop the new potatoes in half if they are golfball-sized or smaller, or cut them into thickish slices, say 15–20mm, if they are bigger. Steam or boil the potatoes until just tender, then add them to the pepper stew for the last few minutes of cooking. The stew is done when the peppers are soft and very sweet. Just before serving, string the sugar snaps, and stir them into the stew with plenty of roughly torn basil leaves. Season well with salt and black pepper.

FOR THE CIABATTA:
1 ciabatta loaf
some pesto or olive tapenade
goats' cheese

To make goats' cheese ciabatta, slice a ciabatta loaf in half lengthways and spread the cut surfaces with a thin layer of basil or tomato pesto, or a green olive tapenade, and cover that with thin slices of strong goats' cheese. Bake in a hot oven, 200°C/400°F, until the bread is crisp and the cheese lightly coloured.

FOR FOUR:

FOR THE TAPENADE:
300g green olives
2 cloves garlic
1 bunch basil
2 tablespoons capers
3 tablespoons olive oil

Stone the olives or pop out the stuffing. Put the olives in a food processor with the garlic, basil, capers and three tablespoons of olive oil, and blend to a smooth thick purée. To use the tapenade as a sauce, dilute with more olive oil.

FOR THE COUSCOUS CAKE:
240g couscous
200mls warm water or stock
2 red onions
4 cloves garlic
1 tablespoon olive oil
200g feta
40g pinenuts, lightly toasted
small bunch fresh coriander, chopped
salt and pepper, to season
2 eggs

Soak the couscous in 200mls of warm water or stock. Finely chop one red onion and the garlic. Cook them for two minutes in olive oil in a small pan, then stir them into the couscous. Break the feta into a rough crumble and add it to the couscous with the pinenuts and fresh coriander. Season with salt and pepper. Add the beaten eggs just before you fry the cakes.

FOR THE PEPPERS:
4 red peppers
1 teaspoon cumin seeds
1 teaspoon coriander seeds, crushed
1 red chilli, chopped
400g spinach

Halve the second red onion and chop it into slices, not too thin. Quarter the peppers lengthways, scrape out the seeds and white membrane and discard, and chop the peppers into slices about 1cm thick. Toss these with the onion slices and some olive oil in an oven dish and roast them at 190°C/375°F for 15 minutes or so. Turn the vegetables occasionally. They are done when both the onion and peppers have softened and caramelised a little around the edges, and are beginning to look a little charred.

Meanwhile, on the stove, heat a large wide frying pan to a low-medium heat. Place four metal rings in the pan and brush their inside surfaces and the pan itself with olive oil. Pack each ring with some of the cake mix, pressing gently on the top of each. Fry the cakes gently for a few minutes before flipping them over. Keep the heat low and flip the cakes a few more times until they are cooked through and the outsides are slightly crisped.

A few minutes before the cakes are ready, heat some olive oil in a pan and put in the cumin, coriander and chilli. Almost immediately, add the spinach and stir it with tongs over high heat until it wilts and takes on a glossy, darker shade of green. Add in the roasted peppers and any juices from them, turn the heat down and wait just long enough to heat the peppers through.

Serve each couscous cake on a generous pile of the peppers and spinach, and put a teaspoon of tapenade on each cake.

Outdoor Cooking

Outdoor cooking

There is a fundamental difference between outdoor eating and outdoor cooking. Our family eats outside a lot, though more because Bridget is a New Zealander than because Ireland has a climate conducive to it. By eating outside I mean that we bring our meals outside to eat in the sunshine (and the rain). Increasingly, we also cook outside. One recent cold evening in early spring, after a hard shift in the restaurant kitchen, I came home to find Bridget and Uncle Ron huddled over the barbecue, a homemade contraption involving the legs of an old sewing table, some red bricks from the garden wall and a thick slab of slate. Every window and door of the house was open to the harsh elements, and Bridget was sipping chilled pinot grigio and frying haloumi. At midnight. Not quite two weeks back from a trip home to New Zealand, she was clearly not yet re-acclimatised. The airspace immediately around the barbecue was the only place not to freeze to death, so I reluctantly joined them.

Generally, I like stoves and grills and ovens and all the paraphernalia of a well-designed kitchen. I like to cook calmly, in the evening when the day's work is done, with a glass of red wine… and a cosy room to eat in. The macho routines of the average barbecue never called to me, the burned flesh and the weak beer and… oh, my god… the apron worn over shorts! But I am a growing convert to outdoor cooking, if not its fashion sense. The first time I gave it any serious thought was a few years ago when I was asked to do a demonstration of vegetarian barbecuing at a barbecue festival in Bantry in West Cork. Sounded like hell to me at first, but the location was beautiful and gradually the challenge grew on me. With a lot of help from Bridget and our South-African cook, Johan, I set about coming up with a feast of vegetable dishes that would cook well on a very basic barbecue. The dishes we cooked that day form the basis of the following section. What surprised me, and what sparked my ongoing and growing interest in outdoor cooking, was that some of the food tasted better than it did when cooked on a domestic indoor stove. Partly because of the very high cooking temperatures and the short cooking times, some of the food cooked in a way I didn't expect. The baby carrots, briefly marinated and grilled, were a revelation. Artichokes and asparagus revealed hidden characteristics. Fennel did not resemble the fennel I like to cook indoors, usually braised slowly in wine and olive oil.

The day was a fabulous success, not only as a food experiment and demonstration, but as a surreal day out in the Irish countryside. Just as we were about to start cooking the main dishes of the afternoon, with a display of the simpler grilled vegetables already laid out to attract attention, a huge black cloud carrying a heavy storm charged into the town square from the bay and drenched everybody before we could look up to point at it and warn each other. We stood around laughing at the predictable unpredictability of it, while some fast-thinking observers scoffed the cooked food, and some of the uncooked stuff as well, in their ravenous panic. Then, out of the downpour, four strong men appeared with long poles. On their shoulders, like a papal procession, they carried the 12-foot long, scorching-hot barbecue across the square and into the fire station, where the demonstration carried on heroically. Only in Ireland… only in the summer…

Although all of these recipes can be very successfully prepared and presented indoors, when writing them down I have focused on recipes for cooking on a simple barbecue of bars over hot coals. A separate solid plate is a very useful addition but,

if you don't have one, it is easy to replicate by placing a thin oven tray on the bars. Some of the recipes do require some preparation of vegetables and sauces, which will have to be done in an indoor kitchen, unless you have a state-of-the-art multi-function outdoor cooking unit, in which case you know more about how to cook on it than I can tell you. Where such pre-preparation is necessary, it is of a kind that can be done well in advance if that suits you best, or just before the final cooking, if you prefer.

With a little practice and experimentation, a lot of recipes can be adapted to outdoor cooking, but an important aspect of food for outdoor eating is that it is durable and flexible. You don't want the kind of food that collapses in an indignant puddle because it wasn't consumed immediately it left the heat of the cooker. The food must be flexible enough to be cooked for five minutes or ten, at 250°C/300°F or 200°C/400°F; dishes need to be good if kept warm at the edges of the barbecue until wanted, and still good to eat much later and cooler when someone gets a fresh appetite, notices they missed a treat or arrives late.

I think there are two different types of outdoor meal, which require different planning and a different approach to the food. First, there is the most common: you come home from work, there is still some heat in the sun and the prospect of a nice, long evening ahead. You decide to eat outside, crank up the barbecue and cook a simple meal, with all the characteristics of a typical balanced meal: one main item, say some simple grilled haloumi or some aubergine sandwiches; some potatoes thrown in the embers and some grilled vegetables, with that jar of chutney your mother left last week; make a nice fresh salad, uncork a bottle of crisp white wine and away you go. In effect, 'dinner', cooked and eaten outside.

The other way that we eat outside is a more elaborate affair where, typically, people gather to spend a few hours eating and drinking. This scenario is nothing like inviting people to dinner, and the food therefore takes on a different role. I would even go so far as to say that it's not important that you choose dishes that complement each other, because people won't eat them in that way. Some will eat a little of everything over the course of the day, others will feast on the three starchy food dishes in one go and eat no more, still others will have nothing but some salad and corn chips. The best approach is to provide as much variety of dishes as you can, keep it flowing as long as it is wanted, and don't worry if someone has mayonnaise instead of satay with the tofu kebabs. I think an ideal menu would have three or four cooked dishes, two or three grilled vegetables, two or three salads, and an awful lot of corn chips and crisps for children and nervous adults.

The quantities I have given in the following recipes are for ten small portions as part of a range of dishes in a party situation, unless otherwise stated. For example, one kebab skewer or two aubergine fritters per portion. These quantities will be enough for four to six people in a more formal setting where you cook only one main dish. They are also easy to multiply if you're throwing a very big party.

Looking through the recipes now, I notice that quite a few are laced with spices or accompanied by spiced relishes and chutneys. It isn't deliberate, just the way they came out, and yet it doesn't surprise me. Spiced food seems to suit outdoor eating, and vice versa, and it suits the drinks that go with a day in the garden: sparkling wines, white wines, ice-cold beer and, Bridget's speciality, real margaritas of tequila, Cointreau and fresh lime juice. Yum.

Roasted pepper rolls of black kale and pinenuts

These pepper rolls make great barbecue food but they actually began life as an elegant dinner dish, served with a cream sauce of lemon and basil or thyme. Hot cream sauces aren't really practical outdoors, so I would serve the rolls with classic basil pesto or a lemony aioli.

If you don't have black kale, use spinach or chard.

FOR TEN ROLLS:

5 large red peppers
250g black kale
80g pinenuts
60g Parmesan, finely grated
salt and pepper, to season

Blacken the skins of the peppers under a hot grill or over a flame. Pop them in a paper bag or into a sealed bowl for 20 minutes or so to cool, then peel off the skin and scrape out the seeds without breaking the peppers. Carefully, slice the peppers in half lengthways.

Bring a large pot of water to a boil, drop in the black kale and cook it for five or six minutes, then transfer it to cold water to cool. Drain it well, squeezing out all the liquid with your hands, then chop it quite finely. Toast the pinenuts for a few minutes in an oven until lightly coloured, then chop them coarsely with a knife. Don't blend or grind them– you want broken and halved nuts, not powder. Stir the pinenuts into the kale with the Parmesan, a little salt and some black pepper.

Place a dessertspoon of the kale and pinenuts along one length of roasted pepper and roll up the pepper tightly, making sure the parcel is well packed. Repeat until all the filling or the peppers are used up. To cook the rolls, brush them lightly with olive oil and cook them on a barbecue, under a grill, in an oven or on a griddle pan, turning as required, until the rolls are browned in places and heated through.

Corn-crusted aubergine fritters with tamarillo chutney

There are so many things to do with aubergines and a barbecue, but this isn't an aubergine book, so there are more left out than included. In a state of indecision, I asked Bridget what her favourite one was, and she surprised me by suggesting this: her mother's standard no-frills fritters, which are usually coated with fine bread-crumbs and topped with a dollop of tamarillo chutney. A woman of simple taste is our Bridget. Unable to leave well alone, and with apologies to Gretchen, I have cooked the aubergines in a coating of corn instead of crumbs. I started by using coarse maize, which I had used previously on various fritters, but after a little experimentation I have decided I like medium-ground corn best. It gives a crisp but not quite crunchy texture. If you can't get medium-ground maize, use coarse, or the original fine breadcrumbs.

Tamarillos are one very good reason to go and live in New Zealand. Shaped like plum tomatoes, they are very often used like tomatoes to make relishes, chutneys and savoury sauces, or served grilled on toast. The flavour, however, is more fruit-like, rich and sweet, though quite acid, which means it can be used in sweet dishes too. Tamarillos make fantastic sweet crumble, which puts them one up on the old tomato. Unfortunately they don't travel well – I've brought in only tiny quantities – as they seem to ripen very quickly after picking. In the absence of tamarillos, use a tomato chutney and promise yourself a trip to New Zealand.

FOR 20 FRITTERS:

FOR THE FRITTERS:
2 eggs
200mls milk
salt
200g medium-ground maize
4 bird's eye chillies, ground
1 teaspoon dried oregano
200g plain flour
2 medium to large aubergines

Beat the eggs and milk together with a pinch of salt and put them in a shallow dish. Sift together the maize, chilli, oregano and a large pinch of salt and put this in another dish. Put the plain flour in a third dish. Cut a slice of both ends of each aubergine and slice the rest of the aubergines into round slices about 1.5cm thick. Toss some of the slices in the flour to coat them evenly. Shaking off any excess flour, dunk the aubergine slices in the beaten egg, and then into the corn. Toss the slices well to coat each fully in corn, then remove them to plate or tray, and repeat the process for all of the slices. Cook the fritters on a barbecue or a griddle pan, or in a frying pan, turning them at least once to cook both sides to a nice golden finish. Brush the hot cooking surface with olive oil before you put the aubergines on it, and again when you turn them.

FOR THE CHUTNEY:
1kg tamarillos
300g apples
200g onions
300mls cider vinegar
half tablespoon salt
1 teaspoon mustard powder
half teaspoon mixed spice
500g brown sugar

Peel the tamarillos and the apples, and chop them coarsely. Chop the onion into thin short slices. Put the vegetables in a stainless steel pan with the rest of the ingredients, bring to a boil and simmer for two hours, stirring, and scraping the sides occasionally. To store the chutney for a few months, fill some glass jars with almost-boiling water for a few minutes, then tip out the water and fill the jars almost to the top with the hot chutney. Screw on the lids and leave the jars to cool before storing in a dark cupboard or in the fridge. Left to cool and stored in containers in the fridge, the chutney will still keep for a couple of weeks.

Ginger-glazed kebabs of sweet potato, tofu and shallots with coconut satay

I probably use tofu more at home than in Café Paradiso these days. Every time you try to create a restaurant dish with tofu, you have to confront the public perception of it and its association with the worthy but dull end of vegetarian catering. Now I don't mind a challenge in work, but sometimes I like to let things go too. Let's say I'm in a rest period in my professional relationship with tofu. At home, tofu is without baggage; it is simply a very useful food to have around. We fry thick slices to eat with spiced greens and rice, toss cubes into stir-fries, float strips in noodle broths; and, best of all, it cooks great on a barbecue. Mostly we grill thick slices, but that's hardly a recipe, so I've opted for this kebab, which combines the salty marinated tofu with the sweet flavours of shallots and sweet potato, and everybody's secret favourite sauce, peanut satay.

FOR TEN KEBABS:

FOR THE KEBABS:
3 x 200g packs tofu
200mls soy sauce
1 teaspoon tomato purée
3 tablespoons fresh ginger, grated
600g sweet potatoes
30 shallots
200mls olive oil
1 tablespoon honey
rind and juice of 1 lime
1 teaspoon toasted sesame oil

Cut the tofu into cubes about 3cm thick, and put them into a shallow dish. Whisk together the soy sauce, tomato purée, 100mls water and half of the grated ginger. Pour this over the tofu to marinate for an hour at least, preferably three to four. Peel the sweet potatoes and cut them into chunks approximately the same size as the tofu. Peel the shallots. Bring a pot of water to a boil and cook the sweet potatoes for about five minutes until almost done. Remove the potato chunks to a shallow dish and cook the shallots in the water for just two minutes, before adding them to the sweet potatoes. Warm the olive oil gently in a small pan and whisk in the honey, lime, remaining ginger and the sesame oil, until the honey is melted, then pour this marinade over the sweet potatoes and shallots. Leave for half an hour.

Put a shallot on a skewer, followed by a chunk of sweet potato, then a piece of tofu, another shallot, tofu, sweet potato and, finally, a shallot. Repeat to get ten kebabs.

Brush some of the honey marinade on to the kebabs, and cook them on a barbecue or a griddle pan, or under a hot grill. Turn the kebabs to cook them evenly and brush a little more marinade over them if they seem dry.

FOR THE SATAY:
juice of 1 lemon
100g fresh or tinned pineapple
half tablespoon grated ginger
2 cloves garlic
2 bird's eye chillies
1 tablespoon soy sauce
150g peanut butter
400mls coconut milk

Blend the lemon, pineapple, ginger, garlic, chillies and soy sauce in a food processor. Pour the puree into a pan, bring it to a boil and simmer for two minutes. Add the peanut butter and whisk slowly while it comes back to a boil. Cook for a few seconds only before pouring in the coconut milk, then bring it back to a boil and simmer for one minute more. If you want the sauce to be thicker, simmer for longer, stirring frequently.

Aubergine and mozzarella sandwiches with fresh green chilli pesto

A slightly more involved dish than the aubergine fritters. This time, the aubergine is cooked twice, or cooked and reheated, more like. I don't think the aubergine will cook all the way through if you make the sandwiches with raw aubergine slices, but, even if they did, the mozzarella would melt all over the grill in the time it required.

The sandwiches are well flavoured enough to be served alone, and any pesto will give them a lift. Mind you, this fresh chilli pesto can easily give them more of a kick than a gentle lift. It's best to check how hot the chillies are before you make the pesto, then decide whether you want to leave the seeds in or not. If the chilli flesh has any reasonable heat, I would leave the seeds out, and you may even want to increase the proportion of herbs if the chillies are hot – the pesto is meant to be fun, not a rugby club post-match sport. Chilli in pesto, or any oil-based sauce, is fun in a deceptive kind of way. At first the oil masks the heat, as do the almonds in this recipe, and then the same heat-carrying oil coats the mouth and lingers for a while. So keep it under control.

FOR TEN SANDWICHES:

FOR THE SANDWICHES:
4 tomatoes
2 large aubergines
some olive oil
2 x 250g blocks fresh buffalo mozzarella
salt and pepper, to season

Slice the tomatoes into three or four slices each and roast them in a hot oven or cook them on a griddle plate, turning once. Cut a slice off both ends of each aubergine and slice the rest of them into round slices about 1.5cm thick. You will need 20 slices. Brush the aubergine slices lightly with olive oil and cook them on the barbecue, on a griddle pan or in a hot oven until just done and lightly browned on both sides. Cut each mozzarella block into five slices. Place a grilled tomato slice on an aubergine slice, season well with salt and pepper, then top that with a slice of mozzarella and another aubergine slice. Press down gently but firmly on the sandwich, and repeat to make ten sandwiches. Cook the sandwiches on the barbecue or in the hot oven for just a minute or two on each side. Serve with a dollop of chilli pesto on top (see below), or on the side for the faint of heart.

FOR THE PESTO:
200g fresh green chillies, chopped coarsely
2 cloves garlic
50g basil
50g coriander
50g ground almonds
250mls olive oil

Put the chillies in a food processor with the garlic, basil and coriander, and blend to a coarse paste. Add the almonds and olive oil, and blend again to get a thick pouring consistency.

Grilled squash with spiced coating

This also works well with sweet potato. A less chilli-hot variation is to use cumin only, or grated ginger with the rind of a lime.

2 tablespoons butter
2 tablespoons olive oil
1 teaspoon salt
4 bird's eye chillies
1 tablespoon cumin seeds
half tablespoon coriander seeds
1 butternut squash, hokaido pumpkin or similar

Put the butter, olive oil and salt in a large bowl. Grind the spices and add them to the oil. Chop the squash into chunks. Butternuts should be peeled but most others have thin edible skins. Bring a large pot of water to a boil and cook the chunks for just one minute, then remove them with a slotted spoon and put them in the bowl with the oil and spices. The heat from the squash will soften the butter. Toss gently to coat the chunks of squash evenly in the spices and oils. Grill on a barbecue or in an oven, turning occasionally.

Barbecued sweetcorn with basil and peppercorn butter

You simply can't have a barbecue without sweetcorn, if for no other reason than to feed the kids.

1 handful basil leaves
1 tablespoon olive oil
2 teaspoons coarsely ground black peppercorns
100g butter, softened
1 ear sweetcorn per person

Put the basil leaves in a food processor with the olive oil, and chop very finely. Add the peppercorns and butter, and blend briefly until the basil and pepper are evenly mixed through the butter.

Cook the sweetcorn ears in boiling water for five minutes, then brush them with olive oil and cook on the barbecue, turning often, until lightly coloured and tender. Put the corn on serving plates and use a brush or knife to smother each ear with the basil and peppercorn butter and a little salt.

Kebabs of haloumi, plum tomatoes and bay leaves with olive and caper tapenade

This time the haloumi is marinated in olive oil flavoured with haloumi's favourite partner, lemon, and some garlic, bay and chilli. The bay leaves flavour the marinade and are then put on the skewers, as much for their appearance as for the lovely smell they give off while cooking. Someone will always try to eat them, of course, but I haven't seen them swallowed yet.

The first time I cooked these, I used cherry tomatoes. They were a little too small, a little too juicy. The plum tomatoes are fleshier and so grill better. The medium-sized Gardeners Delight, or a similar tomato, are good too.

FOR TEN KEBABS:

FOR THE KEBABS:
250mls olive oil
4 dried chillies, halved
5 cloves garlic, roughly chopped
3 x 250g packs haloumi
20 fresh bay leaves
10 small plum tomatoes, halved

Put the olive oil in a jug. Add the chillies and garlic. Cut each block of haloumi in half lengthways and cut each half into five pieces. Put a layer of bay leaves into a shallow dish and cover them with the haloumi. Pour over the marinade. Leave for a few hours (up to 12 hours if possible).

Put one piece of haloumi on to a kebab skewer, followed by a bay leaf, a tomato half, more haloumi, another tomato half, a bay leaf and finally another haloumi piece. Repeat to make ten kebabs. Cook the kebabs on a barbecue, under a grill or on a griddle pan, turning to cook all sides equally, and occasionally brushing on some of the marinade if the haloumi seems dry.

Parmesan and chilli polenta

Polenta is intrinsically bland, but carries flavour well, and this just happens to be my favourite polenta flavouring at the moment: chilli and Parmesan. Not so good with spiced food, obviously, but great with greens or haloumi, or as a snack in its own right, with a cool dip or raita. To serve with spicy dishes, flavour the polenta with fresh coriander and/or lime instead of the cheese and chilli.

1200mls vegetable stock (see page 144)
250g coarse maize
1 teaspoon salt
half teaspoon chopped dried bird's eye chillies
60g Parmesan, grated
1 tablespoon parsley or fresh coriander, finely chopped

Bring the stock to a boil in a large pot, then whisk in the maize, salt and chillies, whisking over high heat until the stock comes back to the boil, then quickly turn the heat to a very low setting and replace the whisk with a wooden spoon. Cook the polenta for 15 to 20 minutes, stirring frequently, until the grains are soft. Stir in the Parmesan and herbs, and tip the polenta out on to an oiled tray. Spread the polenta evenly and quickly using a spatula, or your hands dampened with cold water. In about 20 minutes, the polenta will be ready to cut, but leave it longer if you can. In fact, the polenta can be made up to a day in advance. Cut it into triangles and grill them, lightly brushed with olive oil, on a barbecue or griddle pan.

Grilled sandwiches of artichoke paste, spinach and Coolea cheese

This works equally well with commercial wraps, flour tortilla and soft flatbread like focaccia. The important thing, if using focaccia, is that the top and bottom of the loaf is soft and pale – if the bread is already well done, slice off a thin sliver. I use tinned artichokes to make the paste, mostly for the convenience of it, and partly because it would seem a waste of time, energy and precious artichokes to purée fresh ones. However, if you have a glut of fresh artichokes and you are up to speed with your paring knife, go ahead. The quality of prepared artichokes can vary wildly, and some cheap ones will taste of nothing but the brine they are stored in. The Real Olive Company in Cork's English Market, and in markets all round Ireland, sells very good artichokes dressed in olive oil. If that's not a good reason to visit Ireland, I know a lovely pub that serves the best Beamish stout, far superior to tourist Guinness, and it's close enough to the Cork market to fit into the same itinerary. Coolea is a Gouda-style cheese from mid-Cork, which melts beautifully; would you believe you can buy it in the same market as the artichokes, which is only a short walk from the Beamish brewery? If you're staying home and you can't find Coolea, you need a strong, mature but semi-hard cheese like Gruyère or Gouda.

400g tin artichokes

2 cloves garlic

some olive oil

salt and pepper, to season

400g spinach

1 red onion

200g Coolea cheese (or similar)

8 flour tortillas or wraps

Drain the artichokes and rinse them for a few minutes under running cold water. Put them in a food processor with the garlic and blend in brief bursts to get a coarse purée. Add a few tablespoons of olive oil and blend again for a few seconds. You should have a thick, slightly chunky mash. Season with salt and pepper. Bring a pot of water to a boil, drop in the spinach and cook it for just half a minute, then lift it out and plunge it into a bowl of cold water. Squeeze all the water from the spinach and chop it coarsely. Halve the red onion, slice it very thinly and mix it through the spinach. Season with salt and pepper. Slice the cheese thinly with a vegetable peeler or a wide grater.

Place a wrap on a work surface and spread a generous layer of artichoke paste on it, covering most of the bread but leaving about 3cm at the near and far ends. Place a layer of spinach about one-third of the way up and cover it with a layer of cheese shavings. Fold the near end of the bread over the filling and roll it up quite tightly. Repeat with the rest of the bread and filling.

Brush a little oil on the sandwiches and grill them on a barbecue or griddle pan for a few minutes, turning at least once, until lightly coloured and warmed through.

Sauces and chutneys

Here are four sauces – well, two chutneys, a salsa and a sambal – which guests at our home always lash on to whatever they're served from the barbecue. Barbecues are by nature chaotic, and perfect food combining is not the priority. In any case, these are very versatile sauces. You may have your own, but one of these will add to your repertoire, and your reputation. If I must put a marker down, then the chilli, coconut and pistachio is my favourite.

Watermelon and ginger sambal

1kg watermelon
2 tablespoons sushi ginger or grated fresh ginger
4 spring onions
1 mild green chilli
rind and juice of 1 lime
salt, to season

Flick as many seeds out of the melon as you can and chop the flesh into small dice. Use a sharp knife to avoid squashing too much juice from the melon. Put the melon in a bowl, including whatever juice does escape. Slice the ginger thinly, chop the spring onions very fine, and slice the chilli thinly, discarding the seeds. Mix everything into the melon bowl, with the lime rind and juice, and season with a little salt.

Mango, lime and avocado salsa

1 large green mango
1 mild fresh red chilli
1 red onion, finely chopped
1 tablespoon olive oil
1 tablespoon grated fresh ginger
juice of 1 lime
1 avocado

Peel the mango, slice the flesh from the stone and chop it coarsely. Remove the seeds from the chilli and chop the flesh. Cook the red onion in a little olive oil for two minutes, then add the chopped mango, ginger and chilli, and cook for two minutes more. Put the salsa into a bowl and squeeze in the lime juice. Just before you serve the salsa, dice the avocado flesh and stir it in.

Sweet and hot pepper chutney

3 tablespoons olive oil
1 red onion, chopped into small dice
3 red peppers, de-seeded and chopped
3 yellow peppers, de-seeded and chopped
2 very ripe tomatoes, de-seeded and chopped
4 cloves garlic
6 dried bird's eye chillies
1 tablespoon cumin seeds, ground
2 tablespoons sugar
2 tablespoons white wine vinegar
salt, to season

Heat three tablespoons of olive oil in a pot and cook the red onion for five minutes, before adding the peppers, tomatoes, garlic, chillies and cumin. Cover and stew the vegetables for 30 minutes, stirring occasionally and checking to make sure they're not sticking, until the vegetables are very soft and the stew has a thick consistency. Add the sugar and vinegar and cook for ten minutes more. Season with salt.

Green chilli, pistachio and coconut chutney

150g fresh coconut, grated, or 100g desiccated coconut
4–6 fresh green chillies
4 cloves garlic
1 tablespoon black mustard seeds
200g pistachios
juice of 1 lemon
400mls tinned coconut milk

If using desiccated coconut, soak it in 400mls of warm water for 20 minutes.

Chop the chillies and garlic, and cook them in a little oil with the mustard seeds for a few minutes. Lightly roast the pistachios and chop them finely – but do not grind them to a powder – in a food processor. Add the nuts to the pan with the lemon juice, the grated coconut (and its soaking water, if using), and cook for one minute more. Add the coconut milk, bring it to a boil and remove from the heat. Leave to cool.

A basic stock

A basic stock

Not all dishes need a stock. Indeed, as a younger cook I was interested only in the flavours of the main ingredients of dishes and almost never used stocks. If I felt a dish needed some complexity I put more ingredients in, spices, herbs, oils and so on. What I've come to like about using stock is the layering of flavours that can be achieved. The stock holds a balanced collection of flavours, as one, in the background as a support to the upfront primary flavours of the dish, given by the main ingredients. Think of stock as the bass tone, the element which holds the mood while the main ingredients amuse and entertain. This is important in dishes like risotto, soups and stews.

The title to this recipe doesn't lie. This is the basic model. The ingredients given here will make an acceptable, multi-purpose stock, and they are usually all present in the stocks we use in Paradiso. However, on any given day, it is likely that there will be a few extra seasonal twists. While I don't subscribe to the practice of throwing every spare piece of vegetable matter into the stockpot and boiling overnight, I do use appropriate pieces of cut-offs, leaves and stems of seasonal vegetables. In spring, for example, the asparagus stems are either added to the stockpot, or the water the asparagus is cooked in is also used to cook broad beans, green beans and spinach, and then reduced to a fraction of its volume and added to the stock; or it is used as the starting water for a stock. In winter, I prefer to use celeriac instead of celery, as it has the essential flavour of celery with an earthy tone which is very welcome in winter dishes. Other roots can be used too, though parsnips will add a sweetness you may want to make allowance for. I love tomatoes in a stock for their lovely sweet but sharp nature, but they will colour the stock, so use them only if a slightly orange tint doesn't matter. Most vegetables in their season will contribute a little something to stock, with some exceptions, such as aubergines. Bitter greens and cabbages will dominate a stock too easily, and if you do want to use them, they should only be cooked very briefly.

Herbs play a vital role in deciding the tone of the stock. As well as the basic thyme and parsley, which I would think of as staple winter herbs and use in greater amounts then, a stock in spring will often have fennel and dill herb because I like their airy, heady tone, and in later spring a little of the summer herbs. Basil and, to a lesser extent, oregano speak of the summer and should be used abundantly through the season. Tarragon and sage are powerful but deep herbs that should be used in small doses. I never use rosemary in stock because I feel it is too aromatic and over-powering, but I concede that may be a personal thing, and it's not that I don't love rosemary.

Finally, keep a very good stock powder, or bouillon, handy. I don't like it on its own, but sometimes, if a stock is lacking in depth and dimensions, if you don't have enough ingredients or herbs, add a careful pinch of a very high-quality stock powder and boil the stock for one more minute. The Swiss brand, Marigold, is excellent.

3 litres water
3 onions
8 cloves garlic
4 sticks celery
3 carrots
1 sprig thyme
1 bunch parsley
1 teaspoon peppercorns
1 teaspoons salt

To make the stock, bring the water to a boil in a large pot and drop in the rest of the ingredients. Bring it back to a boil and simmer for thirty minutes. Take the pot off the heat and leave it to rest for thirty minutes more, then drain the stock through a fine sieve to remove all the solids.

Vegetables, by and large, give up their flavour easily and long cooking can cause some to become bitter and old-tasting. A half-hour's simmering and a further half hour resting is enough to draw out the flavour of vegetables, herbs and spices. If you feel you need the stock to be stronger or more intense, you can simmer it again to reduce the volume after discarding the solids. Vegetable stocks need to be fresh, and to somehow retain something of the fresh qualities of the ingredients in them. Don't make stock from vegetables that would otherwise be destined for the compost; your stock, like everything else you cook, will taste of what you make it from.

Acknowledgements

Thanks to John Foley of Bite for the design, Jörg Köster for photography, and everyone at Atrium who was involved in getting the book onto the shelves.

The book is dedicated to the people who produce the food that we cook with: the heroic vegetable growers everywhere, but especially Ultan Walsh grows much of the food that inspires me, both in Café Paradiso and in these recipes; also the amazing cheesemakers of the burgeoning industry in Ireland, especially those who make the cheeses I use most in this book – Bill Hogan's Gabriel, Wolfgang and Agnes Schliebitz' Knockalara, Dick Willem's Coolea, Rochus and Rose's Mature Oisin.

I am, of course, hugely grateful to my wife, Bridget, who supports my writing in the best way possible – by making it seem that the inevitable absentmindedness and general uselessness induced by days of writing (and non-writing) have had no adverse effect on either home life or the smooth running of Café Paradiso.

Index

garlic and olives, 102

see also wild garlic

ginger

gingered sponge fingers, 49

ginger-glazed kebabs of sweet potato, tofu and shallots with coconut satay, 130

in summer squash salad, 68

and watermelon sambal, 141

gooseberry fool with gingered sponge fingers, 49

green beans

green bean salad with olives, capers, cherry tomatoes and a lemon-garlic dressing, 84

roasted, and shallots with couscous and marinated feta, 83

with tomatoes, garlic, orange and oregano, 86

green chilli, pistachio and coconut chutney, 141

green peppercorns

and black kale, broad beans and artichokes with fresh pappardelle in sage butter, 57–8

and watermelon and feta salad, 87

greens

wilted, with roast beetroot, 70

wilted, with roasted globe artichoke, sheep's cheese, pinenuts and tomato pesto, 30

see also cabbage; kale; spinach

grilled artichoke with roasted pepper and basil aioli, 27

grilled asparagus with salt flakes and rosemary aioli, 16

grilled haloumi with lime and mint, 125

grilled sandwiches of artichoke paste, spinach and Coolea cheese, 138

grilled squash with spiced coating, 134

haloumi

grilled, with broad bean salad, wild garlic, lemon-thyme oil and crispbreads, 33–4

grilled, with lime and mint, 125

kebabs of, with plum tomatoes and bay leaves, 136

herbs

fresh herb and feta omelette with warm asparagus, avocado and cherry tomato salsa, 19–20

herbed ricotta stuffing, 66

spring vegetable and herb soup with a fresh goats' cheese ravioli, 45

honey

honey and rosewater baklava, 92–3

ice cream

lavender and honey ice cream, 89–90

strawberry baked Alaska with summer berry compote, 79

kale, black

black kale with plum tomatoes, olive oil, garlic and chillies, 55–6

fresh pappardelle in sage butter with black kale, broad beans, artichokes and green peppercorns, 57–8

roasted pepper rolls of black kale and pinenuts, 127

kebabs

of haloumi, plum tomatoes and bay leaves with olive and caper tapenade, 136

of sweet potato, tofu and shallots, 130

Knockalara sheep's cheese, 10

in almond pastry galette with wilted spinach and crushed potato with tomato-cardamom relish, 42–4

asparagus, caramelised onion and Knockalara sheep's cheese tart, 18

in ravioli with pinenuts and currants, in a lemon-thyme cream, with spinach and sundried tomato, 40

lavender and honey ice cream, 89–90

leeks, barbecued, 124

lemons

lemon and almond polenta cake and yoghurt, 52

lemon-braised artichokes with a white asparagus mousse and tomato–wild garlic concasse, 28–9

lemon chilli oil, 12

lemon-garlic dressing, 84

lemon-thyme cream, 40

lemon, thyme and garlic marinade, 124

lemon-thyme oil, 33–4

lentils *see* puy lentils

lime

grilled haloumi with lime and mint, 125

mango, lime and avocado salsa, 141

mango, lime and avocado salsa, 141

marjoram, broad beans, olive oil and garlic, 37

melon sorbet with honey and rosewater baklava, 92–3

mint

grilled haloumi with lime and mint, 125

mint and chives in risotto of fresh peas, 85

mozzarella

and aubergine sandwiches with fresh green chilli pesto, 133

and organic tomato salad with a warm olive-basil dressing, 94

mushrooms, barbecued, 124

mustard and chive cream, 23

Oisin goats' cheese, 10

shavings of, with avocado and rocket risotto, 12–13

olive oil

and black kale, plum tomatoes, garlic and chillies, 55–6

and broad beans, marjoram and garlic, 37

chocolate-olive oil mousse, 50

lemon chilli oil, 12

lemon-garlic dressing, 84

lemon-thyme oil, 33–4

roasted pepper and garlic oil, 59

summer stew of sweet peppers, new potatoes and sugar snaps with basil, garlic and olives, 102

warm olive-basil dressing, 94

olives

and green bean salad, 84

green olive tapenade, 105–6

olive and caper tapenade, 136

and rigatoni, rocket, broad beans, cherry tomatoes and fresh cheese, 10

tomato, saffron ricotta and olive tart, 98

omelette, 19–20

onions

ginger-glazed kebabs of sweet potato, tofu and shallots with coconut satay, 130

roasted green beans and shallots with couscous and marinated feta, 85

see also red onions